Joy of Life

Joy of Life Publications
8308 Davishire Drive
Raleigh, NC 27615
joyoflifepublications@gmail.com

ISBN 978-1-312-28208-7

An Ordinary Man... A Life Changing Story

An incredibly powerful faith-filled story of how Jerome Friedman, an ordinary man, courageously battled three cancers. During this journey, he experienced an extraordinary gift from God... true joy. This gift left him free from all life stresses filling him with a genuine lasting peace. He humbly shares his story with you so that you may embrace everlasting joy for the rest of your life.

Dedications

To God, with indescribable gratefulness for having taught me how to listen to your voice through your hammering and chiseling, and your guidance in finding the soul of Christ within myself.

To Kathryn - the love of my life, the woman of my dreams, the incredible mother of our children - your spark ignited the *joy* in my life.

To Brock, Vince, Gretchen, and Audrey - your incredible spirit and smiles are endless sources of joy.

To My Family and Friends - who taught me so much through your words but so much more through your loving and inspirational actions.

To Doctor Yoffe, Doctor Schwarz, Doctor Strouch and the other doctors and nurses of Rex Hospital and Wake Hospice - For eighteen years you showed our family the best side of medicine by practicing it from your hearts as well as from your brilliant minds.

To Linda Storm and Christopher Rosaferra - who provided incredible artistic perspective to complete my vision of this project. Thank you for sharing your gifts. The book cover is amazing!

To the readers - in humble gratitude for reading this book. May we together help others experience this incredible, lasting joy.

Contents

Section One
The Birth and Gift of Joy

Chapter 1
The Beginning of Joy

Joy…

On the day the doctors told me that they had found a third cancer in my body, an incurable cancer, most likely leaving me only months, not years, to live, I was still able to find real joy. I smiled and even laughed later that day. I felt love. That day still seemed like such an incredible gift.

How is that even possible? How is it even sane to say those things? Was I living in a fantasy world? Was I in denial about what I was just told? Didn't I appreciate the magnitude of my situation?   No, I knew all too well the realities of dealing with the unimaginable.

My cancer journeys started in September 2010, after hearing that doctors had unexpectedly found colon cancer. That was a shock to hear. Just weeks earlier, I had been told my GI tract looked the best it had in years, that my colitis was finally inactive. Thank God! My life, I thought, was finally returning to normal after 15 years of doing battle with an unmerciful disease - ulcerative colitis. My skilled and wonderfully caring doctor who guided me through this *against-all-odds* recovery, could not believe the news himself. He wanted to have it verified with a renowned pathologist to make absolutely sure the results were accurate.

Doctors said it was almost a miracle they had found this tiny microscopic colon cancer at such an early stage. The good news in finding it so early was that now it could be treated and cured with an almost 100%

certainty. Little did we know then that colon cancer was just the start, an almost easy challenge to overcome, compared to the unexpected twists and turns that lay ahead, changing hundreds of lives forever.

What is the true and lasting imprint we want to leave in this life? Each of us has experienced life-changing events. Some are subtle, where we do not fully realize what has just occurred; others hit us right between the eyes. In either case, we are forever changed by those life events.

My experience was not a between the eyes kind; rather it was of the subtle sort. It started on a rainy evening in 2000. I was driving home with my wife in our car. We had just attended a funeral. Not my first. Not even a close friend, but someone I hardly knew at all. Yet the insights that I had following the service had a profound effect on me. I did not know then that the thoughts I was having would take years to fully form, and that I would draw upon them throughout the next decade in ways that would completely change my life.

My wife Kathryn had befriended a couple at our church, and the husband had died tragically. One of the things that struck me about the funeral was the wide range of emotion I saw inside and outside the church - from a leg-numbing, total-heartache emotion to a stoicism that made me wonder if they knew they were at a funeral. Who was this person who caused people to react in such completely different ways?

The deceased had obviously impacted many, but the wide range of emotions made me think. At my

• • • •

father's funeral, I was entirely caught up in my own and my family's emotions, I was too close to it all. But here was someone I did not really know and had no connection with. The experience allowed me to see something I had missed. Strong words describing this unknown person were missing from the homily. The priest spoke about death, how it affected us, how people tried to deal with the loss, etc., but there was almost no description of the man who had died.

I wanted to know who this person really was. What words would someone use to describe him so I too could know him and share in some way in this wide range of emotion being displayed? What impact did he have on his own life and the lives of others? It caused me to think, "What words would I want someone to use to describe me at my funeral?"

That was it. That simple question never left me. Even years later, the question kept coming back. It would not go away. A voice inside my head urged me to define who I was and measure myself, my life, against that definition. The result was to become what I later termed my Core.

After I had developed the concept and approach to my Core, I started to mentor others to develop their Core. Over the next ten years I kept refining this idea of one's Core as I coached others on how to become who they wanted to be. I realized that I had stumbled upon and developed something that was dramatically changing lives, including my own – an impactful, lasting kind of change. I was molding my life into what I had always wanted and had been seeking but never knew how to achieve.

I started to write a book entitled *Our Core.* I wanted to share this insight and knowledge about how each of us can develop a core, and all the amazing benefits this process brings. But something was missing. I stopped writing. Years passed before I remembered thinking back to my last clean bill of health. I imagined that the missing piece and the test results were proof that my unrelenting battle was winding down.

I had been fighting so long up to that point, it just seemed like the fight would never be over. My mode of daily operation was to just keep quietly fighting health issues as they arose. I smile now because the thought occurred that I had been waiting for something that was not coming; it was just my imagination. "You can let go now," I thought with a sense of relief. Nothing more to discover. Nothing more to understand.

Reflecting back, the cancer journey with all it taught me was the missing piece. All my Writings are the record of discovery and growth that completed my story. Not in any way shape or form did I ever dream that this important discovery would take well over ten years. On the back end would be a three-year unrelenting battle with cancers that would claim my life. That was the missing part I was looking for. It allowed me to share with you a life altering story to help you find the lasting joy I found.

I believe now that all the gifts of knowledge I received from God can help anyone learn how to take all the stress, the worries, the concerns - all of these things which rob us of joy in our lives – away. Forever. Gifts that will enable you to deal with the

● ● ● ●

unimaginable, unexpected challenges in your life that arrive without permission. You will have lasting peace.

As a result of my experience I am and never will be the same. True joy fills every one of my days now. No day is an ordinary day. Every day and everyone I meet each day is a gift. I cannot begin fully to describe what an amazing feeling it is at the end of each day when I kneel before God to reflect and to thank him for all the incredible moments I experienced that day. It seems that each night when I slide off the bed onto my knees that I am thanking Him more than the day before. The joy just seems to be growing stronger and stronger. So genuine! So, motivating! So inspiring! The joy keeps growing stronger and reflects on my face to all those I encounter the next day. It is an indescribable feeling.

I have two main reasons for writing this book: The first is to provide a voice for our four children to help guide them in their lives. My prayer is that reading this book will help them find, learn, and live this incredible, lasting joy. The second reason is humbly to share with others how to experience this joyful point in life. This is a game changer. It is so amazing. It is living, feeling, and knowing each day is incredible. It is simple - I want to help others learn how to bring this lasting joy into their lives to experience all the benefits from having a stress-free life that lasts a lifetime.

Chapter 2
My Story

True lasting effects rarely come from one event. One event may trigger the start of a change, but usually it takes several experiences to provide an opening for our lives. If we are aware of them, they become the motivation to open our hearts and mind to changes that are needed for our growth. These changes in character, faith, and attitude are not a light switch you can just turn on or off; they are more like dimmer switches. They can go up or down to find that level of light where things look their best. Once you learn how to adjust them you will find that perfect level of light - insights into life itself. With practice, you will learn how to illuminate things to be in their best light. This requires real discipline. But, over time, it will be much easier for you to see what you have been missing and how to keep the lights burning just right without ever dimming them again.

Life had been so incredibly good to me. I had achieved almost everything that I had set my sights on. If I put in the effort and brought my best to the goal, there was nothing I could not achieve. I grew up in the land of Vince Lombardi where one learns at an early age that greatness is not given, it is earned. I grew up in a loving family and was blessed with friends who brought much fun to life.

Back in 1983, I received a work scholarship to do post-graduate study in Japan following college graduation. With this global career opportunity, my mind was filled with the possibilities that lay before me. One of the reasons I joined IBM was that I had always wanted to work in a position that had an important international flavor. I had hardly experienced any setbacks to this point in my life. Anytime things did not go the way I had hoped I simply reset and went after my goal with more determination, or a new, exciting possibility presented itself.

I met the love of my life in college. Kathryn Klein. When she finished graduate school and I had a successful start with IBM, we were married in the church we attended on the campus of the University of Wisconsin-Eau Claire. We began our careers in Marquette, Michigan. Before we knew it, IBM transferred me to Green Bay, Wisconsin. There we bought our first home, and I started coaching basketball. After the intense heartache and pain of losing our first child through miscarriage, Kathryn and I were blessed with the birth of our first son, Brock Anthony. He was such a cute kid, with his blue eyes, and just the right amount of curls, and a fun-filled spirit that was contagious.

I love the game of chess. Life for me was a chessboard with exciting possibilities everywhere. All I had to do was develop the right strategy to make life happen. I did not view life as a game, but rather as limitless in real life possibilities. I was having so much fun, and everything was falling into place.

In the summer of 1994, an exciting IBM opportunity presented itself to move us from the Midwest to Raleigh, North Carolina. It sounded perfect - exactly what we wanted. I had the chance to work on a hand-picked team from around the world to generate strategies for my division at IBM. I was being recruited for would help develop the company's global sales and channel strategy.

• • • •

The change was an incredible opportunity, not only in terms of promotion for its global implications, but for a kid who grew up in small town USA, it was global. Whoa! The word *global* was not even being used yet in business. Its predecessor word was *world-wide*. That word alone was filled with endless possibilities and exciting travels. We were thrilled to be moving to a state with family, friends, mountains, and the sea. It seemed perfect. It was appealing with visions of weekend excursions to majestic creations. Heck, just making the move across the county was a new adventure full of excitement.

What I did not appreciate, and way underestimated was the impact the stress of all this change would have on my life: The stress of moving away from family and friends; the stress of buying a new house with a larger mortgage; the stress of moving from what had been home all of my life to a new environment; the unexpected stress of two more miscarriages; the stress of the job not being everything I had imagined it to be; the stress of more financial concern; the stress of rethinking my choices and wondering if I had done the right thing for my family and myself.

Before I knew it, the stress introduced something brand-spanking new - A serious health challenge. Pain. Bleeding. Loss of control of my bowels. What was going on? The pain got so intense that when I went to the bathroom I would bite towels in the middle of the night to avoid waking Kathryn. I thought it would pass. I was wrong. I had to let her know that something was wrong - really wrong.

● ● ● ●

Dr. Schwarz diagnosed me with severe colitis. I remember vividly the doctor telling me that Kathryn and I might never be able to have children again once he started me on a powerful drug to turn the illness around. One week after he first saw me, Dr. Schwarz told me he had to put me into the hospital to give me this drug intravenously. He had to act quickly because he found that my disease had advanced so much that it was putting a lot at risk. The drug's original purpose had been to reduce the chance of the body's immune system rejecting and destroying new organs in transplant patients. Dr. Schwarz added that if my condition did not start to turn for the better after a week of treatment, I would need immediate surgery to remove my entire colon.

What a shock hearing that. It was like having ice water violently thrown in your face. If we ever wanted any more children I had to be admitted into the hospital and have a tube placed in my chest to allow one of the most powerful immune suppressive drugs to flow in. I had one week to turn the corner or go into major surgery. I thought at the time it does not get much tougher than this. I had no idea that this was the start of what was to become an unending, unmerciful, unimaginable 18-year health journey. It was going to throw me onto the most violent roller coaster ride of my life, with unpredictability being its central design point.

I could fill pages and pages with the health challenges I experienced during those years. It just seemed never to end with all the doctor visits, hospitalizations, emergency room trips, surgeries, etc. Each day the colitis provided a strong, humbling reminder of how it would try to break me mentally or

• • • •

physically. If I stepped out of line, and even sometimes when I did not, it just wanted to show me its immense power. I came to know what Coach Lombardi really meant when he said, "...He has worked his heart out in a good cause and lies exhausted on the field..." Suffice it to say, I had been to every major hospital in Raleigh, Durham, and Chapel Hill multiple times. I met more doctors than I could remember. And, because of numerous health challenges that arose from both the colitis and other health complications over the years, I had almost every procedure done at some point that poked, prodded, or invaded my body. All intended to help me keep rolling down the tracks of life.

It would be remiss of me to not also share with you the amazing amount of living and blessings we experienced over those 18 years. After further health study it was determined we could safely try to have children again. That was music to our ears and the answer to our prayers. We were blessed with Vince, Gretchen and Audrey. They were healthy, strong, smiling, and full of joy.

Through all of the trials our faith never left us. It kept growing and teaching. We were blessed with our extended families whose love and support were unending. We developed a circle of friends, fellow church members and neighbors, who became special and important in our lives. I have so many fun-filled memories of family and friends, of adventures back to Wisconsin or down to Emerald Isle beach, all around our country, community and home. Yes, the health struggles were always there popping up without invite, but we continued to enjoy all the fun and drama that life offers: lots of family and friends in our home,

••••

exciting sports seasons and play-offs, classic school plays, seasonal concerts, and talent shows that wowed.

A highlight for our family was our being renewed each week by our St. Francis of Assisi church community: from Masses to picnics, from competitive basketball games to fun activities at Harvest Moon Festivals; from incredible adventures in Boy and Girl Scouts to retreats teaching us how to combine faith and life. We experienced an immense amount of fun, friendship and fellowship over the years, cherished memories. It was great!

All of my health challenges, filled as they were with twists and turns, tried to undermine the faith and character we were all building, but God always provided the strength we needed to endure. He was helping us learn and grow faster than the challenges. Life was good - or so it seemed.

Chapter 3
Time to Choose

It was time for me to choose. To find out what God was offering from this life experience he had given me. To move beyond just being a question and a thought to really reflecting how I wanted to define myself. All I was really doing was posing that question to myself every once in a while. Did I do that just to checkpoint? Was I living a good enough life? Or, was I really going to try to answer it? Was I committed to making the real changes that the question prompted?

The truth was that I did little to search within myself for any depth on this question. Reflect? Why? As I said, things were going well. In fact, almost everything I tried to make happen was happening, and life was good. Actually very good, it seemed.

A question remained from long ago. It was there nagging at me bit by bit. I felt something was missing. On the other hand, I did not want to go looking for it too hard. If I were honest with myself, I would keep myself comfortably protected with those *other priorities* in life. Some of them I thought were irreproachable – family, faith, friends, and work. I did not want to go where I needed to find the true and right answers. So, at times, I would ask the question, "What words would I want someone to use to describe me at my funeral?" But, I seemed to always retain control of the answers, feeling that I was on the right path, living life in the right way.

I have come to realize that I was letting life become a darkness of distraction. Darkness not in the literal sense, but much worse. A darkness that is very hard

• • • •

to see; a darkness that would never let me find the light that comes from true joy. That light I had yet to uncover. That is why I termed it a 'darkness of distraction'. It is comfortable to let things be just the way they are if all is going well. By continuing to live without facing this challenging question, I was letting what I thought should be my life **be** my life. I was a fool.

I was missing an incredible opportunity to open myself to a change designed by God, to chisel me into the person He knew was there. The answers to life were always within me. Now it was time for me to honestly reflect on this hard, character-changing question. To do that, I needed to learn how to listen for the real answers to how I should live my life and to what God saw in me that I was not bringing forth. I thought I was in control, but I was not. I learned being in control was not the right answer anyway. I should never even have had that as a goal. I thought a goal in life was to be happy, but I was wrong. Happiness is actually one of the more powerful distractions because of how great it makes you feel. But, if I was honest and saw things in true light, it was never going to be lasting or satisfying. Why?

I did not have joy. Joy is the right goal to have. Joy sees you through everything. Joy is so much stronger than happiness and connects you with such deeper feelings. There is also strength that comes with it, a feeling that there is nothing you cannot overcome or accomplish when you have joy pumping through your soul. That is when you really start living; that is when life itself starts to happen right before your eyes.

• • • •

When you have real joy, your eyes are truly open for the first time. You see it in every person. You see all the opportunities to engage the life around you. You see it on people's faces. You feel your heart's immense love and how much you can care for each other. You want to give; you want to share; you want to help. Things that never made you smile make you laugh. You get invited into others' souls where their lives exist. They talk to you and share with you their intimate thoughts and feelings. You are honored by that precious gift of trust that is so hard for us to give to one another. You become connected to their lives.

You are living as Christ intended - with eyes wide open. Your heart senses the nuances of other's needs. Your lips share words that touch softly and create a lasting impact with their true and honest meaning. Your ears open to hear things you previously filtered out, but they are enabling you to really connect with others' lives. You are alive with living water that satisfies your thirst for what life is all about. You experience the *Joy of Life*.

I want to share with you the insight that I have been blessed with in my life's journey of discovery. The past years of battling illnesses and life's adversities have molded me into what I always had hoped I might become but had difficulty achieving. I kept wondering, "Why? Why does God continue to let me go through these things?" I got it. I understand now. I changed. But then, like the ironsmith creating his design, I would be put back into life's furnace until I was red hot again with illness or life's cruel twists. I would then be placed on the anvil and pounded with His metal shaping hammer - the sounds of real, lasting change.

• • • •

I remember like it was yesterday when, in 1997, I asked God to take my life as I lay in my hospital bed, suffering from a fever of unknown origin that would not relent. I was in week three of eight. I would go from being so cold that nothing could warm me to so hot I literally had to do a full body ice down. I was drenched from cold, water-soaked washcloths. Ice-filled buckets sat by my bedside for repeated attempts over hours to bring relief from the high fever. Then, as the fever broke, I was so cold you could not put enough blankets on me. This cold and hot cycle would repeat itself every five to six hours continuously over a 24-hour period. It never ended or took a break. My body and mind were being ripped apart and wasting away from the fever. I learned how destructive a fever could be. It was pure torture. It got to the point where I could barely talk or walk. I could not stand any light or noise. It was then I asked God to take my life. But in the morning, despite my prayer, I was still there.

Kathryn brought me a letter that came in the mail that day from my oldest brother Paul. He is a Benedictine Brother who spent over twenty years of his life working with the poor in Guatemala. Paul quoted Mother Teresa as she was holding a dying woman in her arms in a gutter in Calcutta: "How much, how very much Jesus must love you to let you share in His suffering." Suddenly, I saw my physical suffering in a new light. It was a gift. I had been viewing it in a much different light – a burden. But now, I was seeing it as a gift that connected me to my faith and provided me renewed strength for the fight.

My pain allowed me to embrace the cross and to experience a taste of Christ's suffering. I had thought of my faith before as just Catholic. Now I saw it as a faith in Christ connecting me to all of humanity. Christ lived His life to be connected to all people. Almost everyone I have ever met believes in something or someone. I was not being asked to judge others. God does that. God was asking me to love unconditionally. He was not asking me to limit my faith in others in any way. His command to me was to simply love everyone unconditionally. He would do the rest.

God was not done with me by any means. God had much more heating up and hammering to do. He needed me to hear what he was saying that I was not hearing. My learning was not a short term lesson. It was taking years. In fact, when I look at it honestly, it had taken most of my life for some lessons to finally, truly, sink into the fiber of my soul.

The insights I learned now help me to see others more clearly. I hear better what others are trying to tell me. Seeing and hearing life in this way helps me to use my life as it was designed. I want to share my story with you. When you read it, when you hear it, hopefully it will be felt and understood through your own life experiences. Everyone's perspective will be different, because we are all unique. There is no right or wrong way to draw your conclusions from what you read. For me, it was best to let the writing sink in without trying to control the impact. I let it change me all the way to my Core. I believe that surrendering control and trusting in God's plan allowed me to be forever changed in ways that have brought incredible, lasting joy to my life.

There are many life experiences over the years that I could share. Please allow me to share with you two major times in my life that had a deep impact on the

• • • •

shaping of who I am.   First is the life changing development of my Core which started over ten years ago.   Reflecting back, I see now how it was my foundation for it all. With the Core in place, the *Joy of Life* became possible. The second is the collection of Writings sent out during the past three years of my cancer journey. The Writings taught me how to listen to God.   It is in these Writings that the *Joy of Life* was revealed and developed into lasting joy.

As you read the upcoming chapters, I humbly recommend that you keep a journal by your side to record your thoughts. The Core and the Writings are intended to be combined with your own experiences to help you find incredible joy in your life – a lasting peace that lasts forever.

Section Two

One's Core:
Character & Legacy

Chapter 4
A Legacy Defined by Words

Listen for them... in your mind... in your speech... from your family... from your friends... can you hear them?

Feel them... they are there... in your heart... in your thoughts... in your soul... in your every breath... in your yearning... in your passion.

They are there... trust them... they are there.

Discover them... nurture them... declare them... write them down... define them... refine them... know them... let them speak to you... focus on them... be loyal to them.

Strive for them... they are who you can be... live them... especially when no one is watching.

They will never leave you... they define you now... they will change your life forever... they will become your legacy.

Words. What if I told you that a set of words could transform your life into the person you always wanted to be? No amount of money can do it. No level of fame can do it. No single act of luck can do it. No, none of those things create this reality. Those things never last.

What if I told you that these words would last beyond your lifetime? Not only will they serve you every one of your living days, but they will become your true legacy. These words will be a gift to you and to others... especially, to your children. These words will define you, your life, and your lasting legacy.

Words? Yes words.

Transform your life? Yes.

Serve you every day? Yes.

Become your legacy? Yes.

More powerful than money, fame, luck? Yes.

Is that what I am led to believe? Yes.

What words?

How many? Where do they come from?

What do you have to do? Is there a trick?

Your words. You decide. Live them. No tricks.

Is it hard? Yes.

It takes raw honesty and thoughtful reflection.

It will take time.

No monies are ever owed.

Can anyone do it? Yes.

Anyone who thinks and reflects, shows patience and discipline can define his or her legacy.

• • • •

Chapter 5
Developing Your Core

How do you start?

You have to want it.

Really, really, want it. After you establish the 'want' inside yourself, then it is time for real, honest, thoughtful reflection.

Please understand the Core is incredibly straightforward. It is also incredibly powerful because of the changes that will arise in you as you invest in it. True honest transformation. Once you commit, you will start feeling the changes immediately in your thinking and in your behavior. Right away, it becomes part of your entire fiber. You breathe and live it every day. Every moment. It is always there. It does not take any time off. You can be on for ninety nine percent, but when you decide to not be true to your Core, that one percent will be there giving you that raw honest assessment that you still have more work to do.

It is not a game. You are the only true judge. You never fool yourself. Other people are definitely important mirrors and windows guiding you with your Core. Ultimately, you will develop an acute awareness and knowledge of when you are *on track*. This is meant for you. It is a process for truly becoming the person you want to be. With time this process will be so natural and genuine that it will be part of your unconscious state of being. You will always know the true efforts you are putting forth based on the results.

• • • •

Later in this chapter there is a step by step guide on how to develop your Core, but there are some important things to do and understand before you start the process. Please go and find a quiet place for reflection. Close your eyes. Look into the future. Imagine your funeral. All your family and friends are gathered. They are talking about your life, memories and experiences with you. What words are you hearing them use? Are those the words you want to hear when they are talking about you?

You have control. You choose the words. What words would you want to hear?

Realize that ultimately others will try to define you by the words that *they* choose. But, I loved the quote from John Wooden when he said, "Be more concerned with your character than your reputation. Your reputation is what others say about you, but your character is who you really are." The Core is all about character. *Your* character - in your own words. That is why you design your Core, implement it, and judge its success.

There is a clear straight forward path to ensure the words you want others to describe you with are the words you actually chose. Let us say you chose the word *integrity*. From this point forward, everything you do, day in and day out needs to be done with integrity. No compromises anymore.

People need to witness you living your Core words for the words to become who you really are. When people interact with you, your Core words are the concepts they experience. They need to see and hear them over and over in what you say and do. If you

• • • •

want integrity, it cannot be a *sometimes* thing. People will see contradictions in you if you are honest in most situations, but then you decide to gray the truth at other times. Living out your words means embracing Core values at all times.

If you truly want your Core words to define your character, it all starts in the places where you spend time with others. When you are at work. When you are with your children. When you are with your friends. When you are with family. What you say and what you do. How you treat a stranger. How you live your faith. When you talk on the phone. When you are out in public. When you are with everyone. Always.

Why? Because this is you. You do not turn your Core on and off. It always has to be on if it is to become who you truly are.

The list of the words you want to hear others say about you is the starting point for developing your Core. When I began to mentor people on this concept, one of the first things we developed was the following definition of the Core.

> **Core** - A principle-centered set of guiding words that serve as the foundation to develop us as a complete people who are willing and committed to doing the right thing... Even when no one is watching. It is the guiding force and light to help us become the kind of people we strive to be and ultimately, it is our prayer that the Core really does become who we are, intertwined with our soul.

I cannot begin to describe how transforming this was for me. I really let the Core sink into every fiber of my soul. I really wanted to live my life by this set of words and definitions. The words I chose came from very thoughtful and thorough reflection and discussion. I held myself accountable to living the words without compromise.

To help you develop your Core, I put together a list of steps. This process is powerful because you get to choose the words that define you. They will help you become the person you want to be. Reflect on how you feel others would describe you and how you would like to be described. You are now ready to develop your Core.

Step 1
For the next couple of weeks, write down not only all the words that you reflected upon, but also any additional words that capture your heart and attention. Do some research to find inspiring words. Look in areas of interest to find more words. Talk to others and ask for their help in coming up with additional words. Develop a long list of words to consider your Core. Do not overthink anything at this point. Compile the longest list of words that speak to you.

Step 2
From this long list of words, start to pick out the ones that really inspire you. These should be powerful. These are words you would love to hear someone use to describe you. Eventually, whittle the list down to eight to twelve words. One helpful exercise is to group words together by similar meanings. Choose those that inspire you most. For example, I started with over one hundred words on my list. I chose the word

• • • •

integrity instead of *honesty*. I loved the word honesty, but felt it was the foundation for *integrity*. *Integrity* made me feel like I wanted to strive for more. Your final list begins your Core words. These words are those that others would choose to describe you. You are starting to define your legacy. Over the years, I have changed three of my original words as I encountered new and more powerful words to represent what I wanted to develop in myself. For example, I had the word *happy* on my list. When I discovered the word *joy* and understood its meaning, I found that joy better described the person I wanted to be. You find the words that mean the most to you and the person you want to be... at your Core.

Step 3

Write a definition for each Core word. Provide a clear understanding of what the word means in your eyes. You can use a dictionary for ideas, but it is important that the definition is in your own words. The definition should come alive in its meaning when people meet you and come to really know you. Define each of your Core words by how you will try to live it out. This will also show you what you need to do to make it a part of your everyday life. It gives you a road map to make the word come alive in your words and actions.

Step 4

Prioritize the Core words you identified. The first Core word on your list should be the most important to you. The words you choose next should build on one another. There is no right or wrong way to do this. It depends only on what is meaningful to you to give you a sense of what you ultimately are building toward.

• • • •

Step 5

Print out your list of Core words with their definitions so that you can look at them on a daily basis. Not only will this remind you of what the words are, but by reading the definition, you are also held accountable for your performance. This allows you to check if you are living out your Core as you defined it. The definitions will only come true if you live them each day in all you do and say. When I began my Core more than ten years ago, I kept a copy of my Core words in my car, in my office, and by my bedside. I did this so that I had easy access to my list for my daily checkpoint.

Step 6

One month after you have established your Core and have begun your daily checkpoints, take the next step. Pick one of your Core words - whether it is your most important word or a word you are struggling with. Make this word your focus word. This step is a more concentrated focus on one particular word. Keep this word with you throughout each day. For example, I chose my first focus word to be *integrity*. I could feel its presence with every word I spoke. I used honesty within my definition of integrity.

The first few days of focus were a wake-up call. I needed to make changes to make certain that everything I said or did had my definition of integrity attached to it. At the end of each day, I took time to reflect back on what I said or did that day. I would mentally rate myself on my consistency. I was a tough judge. I did not want any grayness to cloud my objective. I began to feel confident in my ability to live with integrity. The checkpoint process became ingrained.

• • • •

Step 7

Continue with your focus word for a minimum of two months - reflecting for as long as it takes until the words becomes an unconscious habit. Your focus word should be ingrained into the fiber of your soul as you live out the true meaning of the word. Some of my focus words took four to six months to become fully ingrained.

Step 8

Once your first focus word has become an unconscious habit, pick your next Core word. Repeat this process until each word has had the opportunity to be a focus word. This process could take a couple of years. This is why developing your Core is not like a light switch. It takes time for your Core words to emanate from you. By fine-tuning your Core with your focus words, you are learning how to illuminate people and things in your life with that wonderful, lasting, radiant light.

Step 9

Pull out your full sheet of Core words at least once per week. Read through the Core words and their definitions. By doing this you are still making progress toward all the Core words while you are focusing on the one focus word each day.

Step 10

When each word on your Core list has been a focus word long enough to become an unconscious habit, take time every two weeks, or at least once a month to reflect on your Core and how you are doing. Keep your words alive and well! If you have been disciplined and followed the above steps, you will be amazed at the tremendous difference you will experience. You will be transformed by your Core words.

Create them. The list will be priceless when you are finished.

Chapter 6
My Core Words

I really love the seven principles that John Wooden handed down to his son John. One of the seven principles was, "Make each day your masterpiece." Having the opportunity to paint a masterpiece with the words and actions we choose is a blessing. A masterpiece is an enduring image which holds a deep meaning for me. I can look at a painting over and over, enjoying it for its unending beauty or finding something new in it from deep reflection. Each time I live in the greatness of its shadow.

Below are the Core words that I used as my daily checklist. I came to realize that I would never reach an end state for my Core. This awareness inspired and motivated me to focus on my Core for the rest of my life. I have received huge benefits from my effort. My Core serves as a powerful, humbling reminder that we are always growing our wisdom to live life as God intends.

MY CORE

CORE: A principle - centered set of guiding words that serve as the foundation to develop us as a complete people who are willing and committed to doing the right thing... Even when no one is watching. It is the guiding force and light to help us become the kind of people we strive to be and ultimately, it is our prayer that the Core really does become who we are, intertwined with our soul.

INTEGRITY	Committed to the timeless moral values of honesty, justice, trustworthiness, etc. free from any grayness of their true meaning and intent. Building a solid reputation where people know they can always trust every one of my words and actions. Removing any question marks in people's minds about my true character and what I stand for and represent.
FAITH	Being open and respectful to other faiths. Having a belief, a trust and loyalty to one's own personal faith and teachings. Living the values and principles of the Ten Commandments through my words and actions. Establishing a strong set of morals and values within my family and being accountable for them.
RESPECT	Treating everyone with genuine dignity. Taking the time to understand who a person is on the inside. Valuing everyone. Showing a strong heartfelt belief in others by demonstrating to them my highest acknowledgement regardless of their position in life.
HUMILITY	Focusing first on others. Celebrating their achievements. Being a true team player. Being unselfish. Removing all arrogance. Living and teaching kindness. Learning from and emulating Mother Teresa & Abraham Lincoln as role models with the ultimate role model being Jesus Christ.
COMPASSION	Full of warm smiles showing mercy and empathy. Sharing your pure love with one's family, friends and all those you are blessed to meet each day. Providing kind, thoughtful, non-judgmental unconditional care and support to others. When necessary, displaying sympathy while trying to understand why others are distressed. Having a sincere desire to help or guide.

• • • •

WISDOM	Having exceptional judgment in making decisions that stand the test of time. Showing a great understanding and deep insight of people and situations. Displaying that unique ability to quickly understand what is happening, discern, grasp important concepts and give sound advice.
JOY	Enjoying each and every day. Seeing people and things for who and what they are. Savoring the goodness all around you. Living life no matter what unimaginable experience life may bring. Having a positive outlook that penetrates to one's soul. Being at peace with God, others, and yourself.
COURAGE	Doing what is right when doing it is not easy. Displaying the moral & physical strength of character to persevere, and withstand personal danger, fear, or difficulty no matter what life may bring into your path. Being confident. Venturing out of your comfort zone to truly experience the gift of life - people and places. Having true heart. Really living life.
LOYALTY	Unquestionable reliability. When I give my word others can depend on me anytime, anywhere, and for anything. A reputation to the point where someone is willing to stake everything, even their life, on my faithfulness to them. Dependable without any doubt... always.
TEAM PLAYER	Displaying an unwavering devotion to teamwork. Putting individual achievement aside. One Team. One Goal. Focused on team excellence & execution of what is possible when all members of the team have success of the team as more important than any personal prominence. When teamwork is so engrained in you that it is an unconscious habit.

• • • •

COACH	Freely giving of your time and talent to help others attain their best. Fostering a culture of execution & excellence. Inspiring individual and team achievement by instilling confidence in all. Always listening with an open ear & an open mind. Building, striving & honing core fundamental skills every practice. Believing, teaching, & living as one team with common goals. Helping the team become 'One' by building the ultimate teamwork possible to achieve lasting success.
GRACE	Unwavering belief & being one in God. Trusting His plans. A calm magnetic charm in all you say and do. Talking with and leading others in ways that are special, appealing and lasting. An exceptional ability to clearly communicate with actions over words. Being passionate and inspirational toward God.

Your Core is the person you are and the person you are striving to be. It is built from the set of words that you have defined you at your Core. The person you want to be. The person you truly are no matter what the situation. It becomes how you lead, how you listen, how you talk with your words and, more importantly, how you act.

Chapter 7
Transforming Your Life

A man's legacy... It lasts beyond this lifetime and, if it is worthy, it is discussed for generations and passed on to others as an example, a lesson, and a gift. Others will learn from it, benefit and grow. Some will take with them a part of it as a priceless treasure that keeps growing in value by making it part of themselves. It is born out of honor, of trust, of heart. It is forged and shaped by challenges few will ever know the depths of, and is tested time and time again by life's unpredictability. It will endure, and it will shine. It is not a right, but what is right. God's strong hand is part of it, but the freedom to choose wrongly or wisely is where many lose their way... and lose their legacy to the wind.

When you encounter a true legacy... You know. You sense it, you feel it, and you know you are in its presence. You feel lucky. Lucky because you know you have just been given one of life's gifts. If you are wise, you will listen, learn, and be grateful to be in its presence.

When a man's head hits his pillow and he closes his eyes and reflects on his day, he knows if he has added to his legacy or not. It is an honor to be touched by someone's legacy... Your Core transforms you when you believe in it fully, work hard to achieve it, and then really live it each day.

• • • •

Section Three
Listening to God:
The Writings

Dear Readers,

Jerome felt that God wanted him to write so others could learn from his experiences and challenges. He posted these Writings to the Lotsa Helping Hands website. When he was unable to communicate, his wife Kathryn would often make a posting to the site.

*This section contains the
54 Writings posted between
October 28, 2010 and July 1, 2013.*

Chapter 8
The Origin of the Writings

Hearing God's thoughts...   It is extraordinary.

How does one know?   How does it happen?   I do not know. I really don't. For me, it simply started one day without any forewarning. It was a beautiful day in the fall of 2010.   The kind of day you enjoyed outdoors. I was finishing with some yard work while walking from our back to our front yard when I found myself unconsciously stopped.   I was just standing there in the yard. Something was different. Very different.   I remember the exact spot like it was yesterday. It was the spot where the most beautiful flow of thoughts suddenly started entering my conscious mind. It was mesmerizing.

They were the most incredible thoughts I had ever heard sewn together, unlike anything I had ever experienced.   No voice, just this tremendous flow of thoughts. What was it like? The beginning of this moment felt like experiencing the most magnificent painting you ever have seen, but hearing it in words instead of seeing a picture, married with the most captivating story ever told in a poetic rhythm of a rushing waterfall.

The thoughts came in way too fast to remember or even comprehend.   It was just one of those experiences in life where I suddenly found myself in the middle of something that I did not, in my wildest imagination, ever see coming.   On one hand, I was trying to determine if it was even real while, on the other, I was trying to absorb what was happening. It was so riveting. These thoughts were just incredible in

• • • •

their meaning and flow. The messages were so captivating and motivating. The impact of it all was so sudden and so powerful. It was so different from my own thinking.

I do not have any idea how long I stood there. I do remember though at one point suddenly wondering if this might be God speaking to me through this flow of thoughts. When that idea came to mind, I stood there more intensely trying to remember what I heard with these thoughts. But, it was just way too fast, too interwoven, too amazing. Any attempt in trying to recall them felt impossible. It seemed like such an injustice in trying to write something down that was beyond description.

Later in the day I did write down a few of the thoughts, but it just seemed so imperfect compared to the way I felt and heard them. The thoughts were so incredible that I had to try to write them down - even if it was only bits and pieces of what I experienced. What I learned to do was to write down those bits and pieces and then use them as inspiration for the Writings. They were my humble human attempt through my imperfect words to share the essence of what I heard.

I never knew when these thoughts would come. They came at different times. In all kinds of moments. When I least expected them. They lasted different lengths in time. They were distinct and powerful. Their presence created an immediate change and impacted my thinking. What I learned to do when the moments came was to let the message flow and then tried to capture later the essence of the thoughts. I could never seem to do them justice. It was impossible to

• • • •

record the entire messages how I heard them. I did my best.

Later times when I was writing, the words flew from my head to my hands and it seemed as though God was helping me to write. It was easy to recognize when this happened. Words came with ease. When I went back to read what I wrote, it was like I was reading it for the first time. I sat there almost stunned as I tried to let the impact of the messages sink into me. Sometimes there was such a feeling of clarity. That was when I felt I had come close to capturing God's intent. At times the interwoven message was incredibly stunning in its power and simplicity.

I was very reluctant to send out the first Writing to let people know what was going on in my life and what we were facing. I felt like I was standing there totally naked revealing my private thoughts, my health challenges, my vulnerability. I did not want to send anything out. I kept feeling a strong hand encouraging me to send out the message. I tried to ignore it, but there was such strength in this hand that would not go away. A strong and simple message to *trust* was revealed. Finally, after weeks of mental resistance, I hit the send key for the first *Joy of Life* Writing.

The responses to the Writings came from people all over the world. Most powerful for me was how others received the Writings. They were received and read in the most variety of ways. Their responses back were as if God was using parts of the Writings to them as a personal letter. Certain words or phrases were penetrating right into their hearts and minds about what they were facing in their life and things that God wanted them to think about.

●●●●

I personally felt God's strong presence. He was taking me, a very reluctant messenger, who just wanted to stay private and still and quietly instilling in me the confidence to keep going. Keep writing. Keep being obedient. The personal, heartfelt responses from others were so strong in their affirmation to me to continue to write with an unfiltered and untethered soul. Each time I started a new writing I never knew what would be said or what direction it would go. I just waited patiently until I felt the right words in my head. The words I heard and began to write were pure with their feelings in an honest attempt to share the lessons I was learning from God.

As the Writings become longer, deeper, more personal, more private, the responses others shared spoke to how their hearts were joining with our struggles. Their words back to us spoke with such powerful meaning about their lives. For some it was about relationships, marriage, parenting, friendships. For others it was about the past, health issues, death, finances, faith, and the list goes on. They were letting the words and this journey flow into their lives by feeling it in their own unique way. It seemed God was intertwining us together in a way only He could.

The responses were humbling to read. They came from people ages five to 102 year olds. There were emails, letters, message posts, cards, drawings, phone calls, face to face conversations. Their expressions were powerful as they described the depth of their experiences and the impact the Writings had on their daily lives.

Expressions of how the Writings were received varied from descriptions of inspiration, healing, growth

• • • •

in one's faith, and changes that were occurring within themselves. For others, they received and shared the powerful feedback or some action one of their family or friends had just done in response to reading the latest writing. It was affirming. There was no doubt that God was in the center of it all. It was powerfully humbling to be a part of this experience. It was clearly showing the immense power one receives from surrendering complete trust in Him.

The following pages are the Writings. They are interlaced with Kathryn's updates of what was happening on the health and home front of our lives. They reveal the powerful change happening within me as I was trying to understand and digest what God was truly trying to teach me. He was teaching me what the *Joy of Life* meant and how to make it last. This journey impacted all parts of our lives. I started to experience the life I had always wanted and always dreamed of having. The Writings are the record of this transformation. They helped teach me how to use this dimmer switch to live in the light God always intended with His design. This was the life I had strived to attain.

• • • •

Chapter 9
The Birth of Strong Whispers
and Thoughts

Joy of Life
(A note from Jerome)
Thursday, October 28, 2010, 3:00 PM

Family & Friends,

Greetings... Hope all is well with you and your families.

My purpose for writing is that sometimes God decides to take our life in a new direction, and that is what recently happened in my life as some of you have started to hear. I am writing you to share that I was diagnosed with colon cancer. Kathryn & I met with the surgeon this past Friday. The first surgery is tentatively scheduled for November 22nd pending the outcome of results from some additional biopsies that were taken from an egg shaped lump in my neck, which recently appeared. We are hoping it is just an infection response from the lymph nodes but should know more in the coming weeks.

The experience truly does bring our faith to light and trust in God's plan. I am at peace because of that trust. My faith has helped me view these challenges as a way to draw closer to God and to try to become the person He intends by using these tests to find the true essence in my life that I have been given. Our faith allows us to step outside of ourselves and see life through a different set of lenses, so when we step back in we can truly live... Not for ourselves but for others... to serve, to love, to embrace the uniqueness in others

• • • •

around us. We can savor things that we otherwise might have passed by. We learn how to create smiles and warm hearts. We learn to really hear the music in our soul and to see and feel God's creation from the sun to the sand.

The blessing is to learn humility with the acceptance that God is in control. To learn how to give without return, to really enjoy who you are - a miracle in God's image. To accept our life, our experiences, and even our challenges. God invites us to embrace. I am optimistic and positively accepting of whatever unforeseen challenges come - the Lombardi spirit is alive and well. Our children provide a fun focus and humor is great medicine☺.

This past Sunday I celebrated a dinner marking my 25 years with IBM. Joining in with my IBM colleagues were Kathryn and our four children Brock, Vince, Gretchen and Audrey. And, as an extra special reward my 96 year old mother came for the dinner along with my brother Mark who had flown in from Wisconsin. It was a fun-filled evening with many laughs and stories. I was presented with a book of letters from friends over the years. Reading those letters was a wonderful reminder of the great gift of friendship in my life.

Thank you for the gift of your friendship and the many fun memories. May you and your families be truly blessed with the *Joy of Life*.

Jerome

Joy of Life – Thank You
(A note from Jerome)
Tuesday, November 2, 2010, 9:45 PM

Family & Friends,

Thank you for all your wonderful notes. Please know without a doubt that I would love to be able to respond to all of you individually to express our family's deep gratitude for your thoughts, prayers, and inspirational notes you sent. I know you understand that there is a lot going on right now, so I appreciate you letting me respond back to you in a group note to extend our heartfelt thanks.

Yesterday, Kathryn and I went in for a follow-up appointment from the needle biopsy that the ENT doctor took from the lump in my neck. The results said to proceed with the surgical biopsy of the lymph nodes in my neck - that will happen tomorrow morning. The needle biopsy revealed cells that can indicate lymphoma so they want to do surgical lymph node biopsies to try to determine what really is going on - hopefully it will still turn out to be an infection response. If not, then we will be meeting with an oncologist to determine how best to approach the two types of cancers. I will be doing outpatient surgery tomorrow at the hospital... which is probably the preferred approach since the doctor will be holding a surgical scalpel around my neck so best that I am completely out and not making any sudden movements LOL☺.

Thank you for your many generous offers of wanting to help in some way. I know Kathryn would be very humbly and deeply appreciative of your help.

• • • •

Kathy Halula, a close friend of Kathryn's, is coordinating dinners, etc. But, please know your thoughts and prayers are truly the best gifts. Our son Vince noticed the true gift of friendship tonight when he commented about the wonderful response from all these people... which let Kathryn and I know he sees and feels the great gifts we can give each other. There are many amazing, inspirational stories out there from people who have encountered life's challenges. The common thread in the stories is inner strength from faith, family and friends... and, yes, laughter. Thank you again for your friendship and wishing you continued joy.

Jerome

Biopsy surgery went well
(A note from Kathryn)
Friday, November 5, 2010, 8:45 PM

I am hoping this note goes out successfully - those of you who know me well, know that I do not know much about computers - so the first attempt at this communication was sent to "No Man's Land!" Here is take #2.

Jerome came through surgery fine on Wednesday (11-3) He was at Rex Hospital a little longer than we had planned. Much to his dismay, his recovery area did not provide pillows - so he was anxious to leave as soon as he could to get comfy on our couch! It was not long before I heard the beginning of *Remember the Titans* being played on the DVD machine!

• • • •

He is very sore (neck and stomach), but has been able to get up to watch some of Vince's basketball practices. The incision was quite impressive (2-3 inches). One of my preschoolers saw him and was very concerned, asking, "Did Mr. Jerome cry? Did Mr. Jerome need to get a shot? Did it bleed?" I guess affirmative to all of the above. Jerome has Derma-Bond instead of stitches, so it looks like he will heal quickly and well. We hope to have some news at the beginning of the week. As always, we are so grateful for all the prayers and support, and friendship.

God Bless~
Kathryn

PS If any of you can fill in for my Jury Duty assignment on Dec 7th... Ha! Can you believe I received my letter on Wednesday, as well?!? Must be God's humor!

Note Out to Jerome Friends
(A note from Jerome)
Monday, November 8, 2010, 4:45 PM

I am including a note that Jerome wrote today. No news on the biopsy yet. Waiting is beginning to seem like a new normal. ~ Kathryn

Great News! I received my annual Green Bay Packer waiting list update postcard, and I am now below the 3,000 number. It only took 25 years to get there☺. It was comforting and a nice distraction to see

Packers play well against the Cowboys and fun to get lost in the game action with Vince and Brock.

Here is a quick update for you - surgery knocked me on my butt for several days - felt like I was on the losing end of a prize fight☺. Mainly I think from the anesthesia side-effects of a pressure headache through the top of my head, sore muscles in my neck from how they had me positioned on the operating table for the surgery, and my abs feeling like I did sit-ups nonstop. I could not sit up without severe pain. I had to roll over and push myself up. It was a funny sight to see how I would contort to get back up from a horizontal position. I learned later my abs went into spasms simulating an extreme amount of sit-ups before they were paralyzed for the surgery. Once I was sitting upright, I was pretty good.

I cannot feel anything from my jaw bone on down below the incision on my neck. It is like Novocain dentist numb which makes shaving a weird and difficult experience. I have cut back on my pain medication during the day which is good and am now just taking pain medicine at night to help me sleep.

We are awaiting results that should come sometime this week. They took out a couple of the lymph nodes and left one or two that were pressing on a nerve that explained the pain in my shoulders and head going into this.

Still doing well mentally and learning to be patient (I'll give him about a B minus ~ Kathryn edit☺).

All my best to you for a great week!! Jerome

• • • •

Joy of Life – Update
(A note from Jerome)
Tuesday, November 16, 2010
Wednesday, November 17, 2010, 6:00 AM

Family & Friends,

On the home front, Brock and Vince returned from Washington DC. They had a four day trip with the Boy Scouts where they had private tours of the White House and Capitol building. They visited 7-9 monuments where one scout gave the history of the historic event and the other scout spoke on the architecture, design, meaning of the monument itself.

Audrey and I camped out in the back yard on Saturday night to earn her final feather for Indian Princesses... woke up to 33 degree weather... she loved it as we played games and read books in the tent. Although we started with hats, mittens, lots of layers she was down to her regular PJ's before we went to bed... she must have Wisconsin blood in her☺.

A phone ringing... an event that happens a lot in our busy home of six☺. The ringing of the phone was just a normal part of the day... until last week. As each day passed, each additional ring became more and more intense with wondering if this was 'the call' with the results. The call finally came at the end of the week, and we met with the ENT surgeon yesterday. We learned 99% of the time the lymph node biopsy the surgeon took out of my neck would reveal what was going on... an infection of a certain sort, a cancer, what type of cancer, etc. In our case, we became part of the 1% of not sure what is occurring nor how serious. They had ended up sending the biopsy up to Mayo

• • • •

Clinic for additional analysis.   Their findings were suspicious for lymphoma but because there was such extensive necrosis of the tissue it prevented a diagnosis and thus set up a meeting with an oncologist.

We met this morning with Dr. Mark Yoffe, an oncology specialist, who deals in treating patients with lymphoma, leukemia, melanoma, and other forms of cancers and blood diseases.   His goal now is to do additional tests to try to determine if this lump is cancer and, if it is, what type, what stage it is in and if there are any other cancer areas in my body.   There are over 30 types of lymphomas so it can run a wide range of not too serious to more challenging. They drew quite a bit of blood today and later this week they will do PET & CT scans and potentially a bone marrow biopsy to hopefully determine what and how best to approach treatment.   Right now the colon cancer surgery will be delayed.

The feeling I had when the phone rang each time last week was that I was being taught how to surrender, to be patient, to have complete trust. It was not easy but a powerful lesson. I was learning how to wait and how not to. I learned how not to waste time or energy on that which we really do not control. Our faith can truly try to teach us, if we let it, to learn how to surrender, be patient and trust, but ultimately we must make that difficult choice to really trust and let go. If we can do that it provides wonderful gifts in return of lasting joy, love, and contentment with all that we have... and the phone rings are enjoyed once more. There is no more focus then on 'I wish this...' or 'I want that...' It is replaced by an appreciation and an awakening of all that is already around us... embracing life and all of its amazing gifts. Thank you again for

• • • •
68

your friendship. Wishing you and your families continued joy.

Jerome

P.S. A cute story to share... While Kathryn & I were waiting in the ENT's office for the doctor to come in, our dear six-year-old Audrey tore out a 4 x 5 inch note out her little notebook and handed to me. It read, "To Dad, I hope it goes well! Love, Audrey." She did not have a clue what it was all about yet she knew the perfect thing to say... An amazing gift from God.

Kathryn learns how to send the emails!
(A note from Kathryn)
Wednesday, November 17, 2010, 5:00 PM

Thank you Karen and Kathy for letting me know that I needed to press 'email' on the bottom of the message board! Now you ALL may get the updates☺.

Today Jerome had his CT scan and survived the nurse's comments, "You might experience a metal taste in your mouth, you may feel a warm sensation all over your body, and you may feel like you have to go to the bathroom!" Those are things you should NOT tell a patient! Of course, that was all he could think about as he went through the procedure!

Now we are sorting through the massive amounts of paperwork from just the diagnostic work-ups. Yikes the open biopsy alone was incredibly expensive! We have NO DOUBT met our deductible already!

• • • •
69

Thanks again for all the support!

Kathryn

November 18, 2010
(A note from Kathryn)
Thursday, November 18, 2010, 11:15 PM

Good Evening! Jerome's colon surgery is tentatively scheduled for December 16th at UNC. This surgery date is pending the results from his PET scan which he will have tomorrow morning at Rex Hospital and the results from the CT scan which he had yesterday. We look forward to getting some answers and making a plan. Thank you for your continued prayers, support, and reminders of what we are truly thankful for family and friends like you!

Peace and good things to you all,

Kathryn

Happy Thanksgiving
(A note from Kathryn)
Tuesday, November 23, 2010, 8:15 PM

Well, after a week of uncertainty and waiting, we talked with the oncologist last evening. He reviewed the results of the CT and PET scan with us. He was concerned about an intense hyper metabolic mass on Jerome's tongue. We were referred to an ENT surgeon who specialized in this area. Dr. Meredith met with us this morning and ordered another CT scan and another biopsy (to be at WakeMed on Monday, November 29th). We look forward to getting feedback on this biopsy. Possible results are - lymphoma, squamous cell cancer, or infection/benign cyst. We are praying for the best outcome. We still have colon cancer in early stages. All else on the scan looked good.

With a few days off I am taking the girls to Eau Claire, Wisconsin to see Grandma Rosenow (soon to be 95) and Grandpa Klein (soon to be 101!) in Cochrane, Wisconsin. Please continue to pray for safe travel for us and good results on Monday's biopsy. The boys and Jerome will spend Thanksgiving with Jerome's sister, Joan and his mom here in Raleigh. Vince is making two pies! I will return on Monday.

Jerome's spirits are good. He is strong in his faith. We are ready for a 'plan' and some action!

We are thankful for each of you in our lives. May you all enjoy your family and those you love this Thanksgiving.

Peace,
Kathryn

• • • •

Joy of Life – Unknowns
(A Note from Jerome)
November 28, 2010 10:14 PM

Family & Friends,

Greetings. I hope those who celebrated Thanksgiving had a wonderful time... what a great holiday!

Unknowns... Tuesday night last week the oncologist called our home to let us know that the results of the PET scan revealed an intense hyper-metabolic mass on the back part of my tongue. Instead of visiting with him the next day as planned, he asked us to go meet with an ENT oncologist surgeon the next morning. When we met with him, he felt a mass on the PET scan might just be a benign cyst, but he also found a new swollen lymph node which unfortunately meant, to be safe, going back into surgery early tomorrow morning. He will examine everything very carefully inside my throat when I am totally out and then take a new surgical biopsy of this swollen lymph node so he can hopefully try to rule out lymphoma or other cancers.

Unknowns... My mother shared with me last week some family history I had never known. It turns out that my great-great grandfather came to America in 1835 from Germany. Wow, I knew we came over long ago but never knew exactly when. When he came over at the age of twenty, I can only imagine the amount of unknowns he faced. This thought has given me a great source of strength thinking about his courage and the attitude he possessed to accomplish what he did.

• • • •

Anton Anthony Friedmann lived to be 86 passing away in 1901- amazing longevity for back then. I really loved finding out though that he met his wife Elizabeth in America and was married to her for 58 years until she died in 1893. They were a good Catholic German family who had eleven children. Their life I know was not easy. They endured the heartache of losing three of their children before they died themselves.

What I am going through I won't kid you is not easy. There is a mental and physical toll. But, so many people before me in this world have faced greater unknowns and greater challenges. It is in their lives, in their attitudes, and in their joys that I find great strength in my faith and trust in God. The final point to share on my great-great grandfather is that when he died the write-up about his funeral said, "Mr. Anton Friedmann was one of Liberty Township's most highly respected citizens, always a devoted husband, and as a neighbor always kind to oblige." Well then, to continue to honor his legacy, I guess I have a lot of living to do to try to live up to the reputation that he set back in 1901.

Wishing you and your families the continued joy of life ~ even with all the unknowns we all face...

Jerome

Biopsy News *(or lack thereof)*
(A note from Kathryn)
Monday, November 29, 2010, 8:00 PM

Happy Belated Thanksgiving! The girls and I took advantage of a 6 day break from doctor commitments and went up to Wisconsin for a quick visit to my grandparents. It was a fabulous visit - all too quick. Gram is doing very well. We are all sad to be cleaning out the house, but together the task is a bit easier. Grandpa Klein still has his sense of humor and enjoyed a fashion show put on by his great granddaughters! The trip home went quickly - only 14 hours with little to no traffic. What a difference from last Wednesday when we bonded with 15,000 or so of Chicago's finest during a two hour back-up in the windy city! Whew! The freezing rain also added to the excitement!

Today Jerome had a biopsy on the mass that was identified on his tongue last week. The surgeon also took a biopsy of a large lymph node on his neck (above the previous biopsy location). We have no immediate results. The surgeon gave no indication on what the results were leaning toward. Jerome's sister Joan was with Jerome, and she pressed the surgeon for some answers and insight. He did not indicate any possibilities. We were told that they may know something from 48 hours to a week time frame. We have been in this position before - so we will wait and pray. Please join us in this journey!

Jerome is in some discomfort. His throat is quite sore, and he is eating soft foods for the next three days. This new incision is covered, and we are not to touch it until he goes in on Thursday, so I am not sure

••••

what it really looks like. Will let you know when we know some news.

Love,
Kathryn

Side note from Kathryn
(A note from Kathryn)
Wednesday, December 8, 2010, 9:45 PM

We finally received news on the biopsy. Jerome has lymphoma. He is in good spirits after watching Vince's varsity team play an incredible basketball game last night in Durham. Jerome is psyched and ready to 'play' to win in the game of LIFE.

Tomorrow we are planning to go to Rex for the first cycle of Chemo. The oncologist gave us a tentative plan for the treatment. First cycle will be three weeks at Rex Hospital. Jerome will return home for a week or so until levels are stable, and then go back to the hospital for a week. He can come home again for a week or two till his levels are stable, and then it is the home stretch for 3 weeks again in the hospital. If the bone marrow biopsy returns positive, then one additional cycle would be tacked onto the end of our existing plan, but the doctors are not leaning in that direction at this time. We are encouraged by the statistic that 60-80% of the patients are cured with this aggressive treatment. The chemo will not have an effect per se on the colon cancer, so when all is said and done with the lymphoma, we will tackle the colon. We will take it one step and one day at a time.

• • • •

We are overwhelmed by the kindness and great efforts of those around us. The meals and help have been tremendous. Our journey is a long one ~ Thank you for all the continued prayers and support!

Love to all,
Kathryn

Chapter 10
Joy, Reflections, Struggles & Lessons

Joy of Life – Audrey's Joy
(A note from Jerome)
Thursday, December 9, 2010, 10:30 AM

Family & Friends,

My heartfelt and fun thoughts are with all of you for a great time celebrating your religious traditions with your family and friends and for a joyous time bringing in our New Year of 2011.

Wow! The news from our oncologist doctors at the end of last week brought the diagnosis of lymphoma. During the surgery last week they ended up doing two biopsies. One, where the PET scan showed the hyper activity mass and another one on my neck for the lump they unexpectedly found under my jaw. Both areas showed lymphoma. We met with the lymphoma oncologist on Tuesday this week and received the diagnosis.

It is a highly aggressive large B cell high-grade unclassifiable lymphoma. More pathology is being done, but this will likely remain the diagnosis. My cancer cells are growing at a rate of 97-98 on a scale of 100. Unfortunately, this is not a cancer where time is a friend, and if left untreated the cancer will most likely take one's life in about six months but no more than a year. So, I am headed into the hospital today for three weeks for the first round of the most aggressive chemotherapy they have developed for lymphoma. Because of the complexity, precision, and intensity of the chemotherapy protocols it must be

• • • •

done as an inpatient in a hospital setting. Then they can provide the vital round the clock care and complex treatment that must occur to try to achieve success. This is a very rare lymphoma and very complex aggressive treatment.

Today when I arrive at the hospital they will start giving me my first chemo treatment - four drugs. Before the chemo, they will take me into surgery and insert a double Hickman port into my chest. The chemo drugs rip up normal IV lines. Once the port is placed, the first chemo drug will be dripped in. Drugs two and three will be pushed into my body quickly with a syringe. At the end of the day, they will have me curl into a fetal position as they puncture my spine with a long needle to withdraw four tubes of my spinal fluid. They will replace the spinal fluid with precisely four tubes of a chemo drug meant to kill any of the cancer that could be in my spinal fluid or brain tissue. It is a very delicate procedure with severe side effects.

I went in yesterday for the tests on my heart, and all looks good so I should be able to endure the effects of the treatment - bring it on☺. The colon cancer surgery is indefinitely postponed until we can first achieve success with the lymphoma. There is a silver lining. Because this is such a fast growing aggressive lymphoma it really soaks up the chemotherapy medicines. If your body responds, there is a high cure rate. I am without any fear, and I am ready for this fight.

The only tough thing for me was when the kids each realized that I would not be home for Christmas. I saw sadness in their eyes and heard sadness in their voices. The early Christmas blessing is the strength I

• • • •

see growing in them and their appreciation for life. Please see the PS at the end of this note if you would like to continue to receive and read future updates as this is my last update I will be sending. All future updates will come out through Kathryn's email ID for awhile.

My faith has filled me with calm and positive strength that feels no limits. It does not feel as a passing fleeting euphoria but rather the deepest strength I have ever known. Although I have been a very reluctant author of these emails, the writing has stripped away all self. Inspired thoughts and let me know this never was about me, my illnesses, or the challenges I face. It was all about the meaning of this journey and the insight it has brought. I humbly share with you and hope there can be some benefit. Your many responses have told me my notes have struck a real chord in many of you. For that, I swallow my own desires and am grateful to God for his inspirational thoughts given through this experience. The gift to me is limitless faith that has given me no fear, no worries, no concerns. The chance to go through this early hell in my life is a chance to strip myself of everything I need to let go of and truly trust the Will of God.

The message has been clear to me - it is to live. Not exist, but to live. Really savor life. Each day is filled with so many moments. Some we plan, some are unexpected, and there are a lot in between. We truly have been given the gift of life. It is so precious. It is so amazing. There are so many possibilities.

Life took on new meaning early when Kathryn & I lost our first pregnancy. That was life. It was the life of our child, and it was painful. I would have and still

• • • •

would do anything to have held that child just for one moment - to hold that gift of life in my hands, to see our child with my eyes, to kiss him or her with my love. Life. It is so precious. Each life. Savor life. Live each day.

For me, you can take the Bible and break it all down to one word. Love. It is not 'love those you like' or 'those you are comfortable with' or 'those you are close to'. It is love. I deeply respect all faiths. I have learned so much from my friends from all walks of faith. Mine is not to judge one to another. I am just grateful for my faith. My role is to respect others in theirs and learn from them. The most common element of all is 'love'.

In my faith, I was given an amazing example of love. Christ's example in my life is the greatest single act of unconditional love to emulate. It is not complex, but it is so very hard to do well. The strength it takes to love those that strike at you is one thing, to love after what Christ went through is another. I aspire each day to love all those around me... No matter what. It is my faith without excuse and exception.

I love coaching. I love helping children find confidence in themselves to do new things and build momentum for their lives ahead. My coaching role model is John Wooden. In all of my time in doctor's offices and waiting for test results,   I have been reading two books - John Wooden's A *Game Plan for Life* and Mother Teresa's *No Greater Love*. Tremendous books. The book selections were not intertwined when I checked them out from the library, but it was a wonderful surprise to read how they came together, the greatest coach ever and a modern day saint. I

• • • •

discovered it when John Wooden devoted a whole chapter to one of the seven mentors in his life - Mother Teresa. He made me reread this chapter countless times as he said the Mother Teresa quote that stayed with him was, "Unless a life is lived for others, it is not worthwhile." Wooden wrote, "Each of us has a responsibility to lead our life with a focus beyond ourselves... Life should be a complex network of relationships and encounters that all serve to grow an individual and others."

Living your life for others. When we live our life for others, I find I also need to forgive. No one is perfect. Things are not always going to go the way we would like. Life brings all kinds of twists and turns. One of the greatest feelings is to forgive someone. I learned that there is no grayness in forgiveness. I learned that humility is one of the greatest strengths a person can possess to teach you when to discover the many opportunities to forgive. The toughest person to forgive often is yourself.

I have heard what I am about to go through will want to make me literally crawl out of the room. My doctor did not sugar coat it and told me I would go through hell before it got better. But, I'm smiling. Why? I love to laugh. It is the greatest feeling. I laughed and said to my doctor, "So you're telling me that my reward at the end of this treatment is colon surgery?" I just smiled and laughed.

One of the best things that happen when my family gathers every two years for our family reunions is the laughter we share. It truly is the best medicine. These times are a great renewal, but I have learned joy is always there. I have learned joy is the level to aspire

• • • •

too. For it is always there because of the gift of faith. I am not happy for these illnesses or the challenges, but I am joyful for the multitude of gifts from God starting with all of you. You have helped me to trust, to live, to love, to forgive, and to laugh.

My 96-year-old mother said it best to me when I was writing this last note to you. I told her that I would be taking a very long break to focus on the treatments. "That's good. You have said enough," She said with a smile on her face, a chuckle in her laugh, and a kiss on my cheek.

Thank you for your friendship in my life. We have told our children the best thing they can do is to focus on living their normal lives. Just play, learn, and laugh... a lot. May you and your families be truly blessed with the joy of life.

Love and our best wishes to you from the Friedman's ~Kathryn, Brock (17), Vince (12), Gretchen (11), Audrey (6) & Jerome

PS Audrey's Joy - A coaching friend captured our 6-year-old dear little Audrey perfectly in a recent game of hers. Her spirit of joy (so beautifully represented on the cover of this book) is exactly how I feel going into this. Thank you, Todd for truly capturing this *Joy of Life* moment.

My son Brock I think also captured the spirit of joy a child can bring when he wrote a short answer essay response for his University of Notre Dame application, "The innocence of a child is an incredible thing. Their minds spawn fantastic creations when their imaginations run wild. Combine the purity and

• • • •

imaginative talent of a child and a wonderful person is made. Whenever I work with small children, they are always full of smiles and fun energy. Perpetual curiosity fuels them, and they always thirst for more knowledge and exploration. I love seeing the joy in kid's faces when they discover new things or ponder a new idea. It always reminds me to stay young at heart and possess an open mind."

Brock, you nailed it. I have learned so much joy from you, Vince, Gretchen, Audrey, and Kathryn.

Love you!
Dad

Jerome Ready for the Game!
(A note from Kathryn)
Thursday, December 9, 2010, 10:15 PM

Jerome got a Number 2 buzz cut today. It looks great! He said he wanted to strike first before the cancer did on his hair. I am going to try to snap a picture or two tomorrow. He is 'training' at the hospital for the next three weeks. Great room. In fact, when I told Gretchen about the room, she asked, "Sunshine?" Well, not quite the best view, but there is a great big window with nice natural light. Now that you all know where he is, my notes may be shorter and every few days, unless something out of the ordinary occurs.

The kids and I will be bringing a tree (Thanks Ms. Nancy) and some decorations tomorrow. He is in good spirits. The food is good! The food at home here has

• • • •

been wonderful. Thank you to all the great chefs this week!

Peace,
Kathryn

General Information
(A note from Jerome and Kathryn)
Saturday, December 11, 2010, 11:15 PM

Dear Family and Friends,

Thank you for the many wonderful, inspirational, and encouraging notes so many of you have already sent. We will continue to read the notes you send, but Jerome is trying to stay off the computer and rest. Our friend Steve hooked up the NFL package to his laptop this afternoon, so he is ready for the Packer game tomorrow. Some things NEVER change☺.

All future updates will only come through the *Lotsa Helping Hands* website which supports families in need.

Jerome's mental state is amazingly calm after his first chemo treatment. One look in his eyes quickly lets one know the depth of his strength and real love he has for people. He is joking with everyone and keeping spirits up for those around him. He has quite a bit of pain in his legs. Not sure why, but he has done much walking the past couple days all over the hospital. He went outside several times to breath in some fresh air and feel sunshine. He got stopped once, but just found

• • • •

another door to get out as he said the outside air and sunlight are great medicines for the soul.

He sends his very best to you and your families for a wonderful fun filled weekend - feel and live the joy!!!

Love,
Kathryn

Jerome is on track
(A note from Kathryn)
Wednesday, December 15, 2010, 10:30 PM

I just wanted to thank all you 'Meals on Wheels' people out there! The treats (and well-balanced meals) have been fabulous - and so appreciated. Kathy and the Preschool have been very supportive and have let me get out each day quickly to get up and spend time with Jerome each afternoon before the Friedman tribe arrives home. Thank you for helping me maintain normalcy for the kids. All of the prayers are a blessing. They are keeping me going.

Jerome has remained very positive as his treatment course becomes more challenging. He has pain in his jaw, ears, and mouth. He continues to walk as much and as far as he can tolerate to keep the chemo circulating throughout his body. His hair is still growing as evidenced by a minimal bedhead look☺. The care he is receiving is wonderful. All the nurses are exceptional people!

• • • •

A few special moments this week...

We enjoyed a Packer tailgating party in our room on Sunday with great Packer Backers, Scott, Joan, and Jerome's mom, Louise! Fr. Bill joined us midway through the game and prayed with us for healing. He must have had an insight into the outcome of the game!

Jerome continues to minister at Rex with his IV pole in tow. Jerome prayed with a woman and her daughter on another floor. The next day the woman saw Jerome and gave him a big hug and kiss!?! And thanked him for the time and prayers - her husband was showing a little improvement!

Jerome aided a gentleman with a broken leg get into his car outside (must have been a record cold day here - in the 20s)... while he was doing that his IV machine beeped and signaled that the temperature outside was too cold! He joked with the nursing staff that he needed anti-freeze! Jerome really cares about all the people he is coming into contact with - custodians, nurses, aides, physicians, patients, etc. He takes the time to say their names, introduce them to the family, and enjoys their presence in his day.

Jerome has a two-day break from treatment. The nurses and doctors are monitoring him closely. He is very tired, so our family visits are very short, but we are able to talk on the phone - and the kids can say good morning and goodnight. Kenna misses Jerome... for the first time she slept ALL night on the bed with me! I felt like I was at my Aunt Joan's in Milwaukee with Emmie! I am in good paws!

••••

I know Jerome was taking time today to put together a note that I will forward to you all perhaps tomorrow. Please know how much we appreciate your prayers, rides for the kids, and offers of help!

The Monkey classes had our preschool Christmas programs the last two days. "We're Gonna Take a Walk to a Place That's Blessed and Holy..." The kids sang loudly and clearly as they traveled to Bethlehem. The three-year-olds demonstrated that they 'got' the story of Christmas... May you all be blessed to, "Get it, enjoy it, and pass it on!"

Love,
Kathryn

Joy of Life... Raw & Real - My Christmas Letter
(A note from Jerome)
Saturday, December 18, 2010, 7:30 PM

Family & Friends,

It just burns. Reflecting now, it seems appropriate that the harshest effects of the chemo start in my mouth. In the middle of one of the early nights this week, my tongue, then my gums and then my jaw and lips were suddenly aflame. It just burned. My mouth has come alive with the fire of first cleansing that is now serving as a living reminder of how words can wound. But, it is a bright future as this experience reminds me of the multitude of opportunities I have each day to heal going forward by bringing forth words to others that really encourage and nurture their day.

• • • •

I could write a 1000 stories of what I have experienced since this began. Let me start with one where I told my mother the news. As I held her hands and looked into her eyes, I told her as gently and honestly as I could that we now know this newest cancer to arrive is lymphoma. I shared that they were doing more tests to understand if it was this more rare type and that would tell them how best to treat it. I could see her fighting for the strength she felt I needed to hear and then gave the honest, loving response of, "Oh Jerry, I thought God would hear my prayers..." God gave me a quick response for my mother when I said, "I think He did Mom. He is just giving us different answers and asking us to fully trust in Him." Isn't that what gives strength to the meaning of the word faith... *trust*?

Trust is what has allowed me to let go. I turned over my entire retirement fund I managed for over 25 years in about 30 seconds to my friend Steve who offered to help. I also gave him the names of Ken, Jim, and John - three other friends I just knew could and would be right there to help him with their unique skills. That is what makes friendship amazing. To know you do not even need to call and ask. It is just there.

My friend Scott joined my 96 year-old mother, my sister Joan, Kathryn, Vince, Gretchen, Audrey and I to watch the Green Bay Packers game on Sunday in my hospital room. Just an ordinary day. We stopped in the second quarter when Fr. Bill arrived. He was bringing me a special blessing of the Sacrament of the Sick. It was the first request of my mother to me to have done. It meant a lot to her. So, after he blessed me, I asked him if he would please also anoint her. It was such a life moment. Family and friends gathered. United.

••••

Praying. Laughing. Sharing each other's company in odd transitions that was life itself.

Scott shared in the afternoon. He is a former professional athlete who gave me his signature... not his name written on something. No. His signature was the depth of friendship he wanted me to understand. His sister had a different type of lymphoma and now works at the Stanford Cancer Center. Upon sharing with her what was going on with me, he just wanted me to know that in a *Brian's Song* real-life moment he was there for me. It is a symbol of how Kathryn and our family feel for all of you. We value your friendship and your list of names on the *Lotsa Helping Hands* website. It is so wonderfully refreshingly 'raw' & 'real'.

As Scott and I spoke, we gave each other a private commitment. Making commitments build friendships. Both of us will be changed forever as a result of living out those commitments, and that is what makes the word friendship one of the most meaningful words in my vocabulary.

Kathryn and I are humbled by all the names on the website. It has been true joy seeing your names there and old names from long ago popping up. That is a gift. I could tell countless stories. Where I have seen you. What I have seen you do. What I have learned from you. I saw the name of Bob Kinzy who first hired me into IBM 25 years ago. I remember like yesterday when I first met him. He had a warm, welcoming energy and excitement for the possibilities of the future.

This IBM tradition was carried forth by the first visitor to my hospital room - Rick Jordan - my current

IBM manager. He was there first as a friend and then to let me know that he was there for Kathryn 24 x 7. Those were not just words as I shared with Kathryn. He meant them. He graduated over 30 years ago from West Point. He is a rock of honor that men and women in uniform represent. He and Bob represent the best about values and qualities of leadership. They work within a company where tradition and our country's values are at its core.

Then there is my friend Assan. I did not realize what a gift he was until just before my first cancer diagnosis, but he gave me a great gift. Assan is an 80 some year-old man whom I met in yoga therapy. I saw him twice a week for a long time, and we were always quick with our smiles to each other and wishing each other well. On one particularly tough day I shouted to my friend the normal, "How are you today?" His answer was the same, "No Complaints." But, for the first time in over a year, I really heard it. I was dumbfounded. He really meant what he was telling me. He had no complaints.

As this thought was sinking into me, I walked quickly across the room to him, and I said, "Assan, some day you need to share with me the wisdom on how I can give an answer like that too." Assan suddenly got serious. He looked deep into my eyes and said, "You have heard of Gandhi?" to which I replied, "Yes." He said back in the 70's, Life magazine had done an interview with Gandhi and asked him, "Why is the West so unhappy?" To which Gandhi replied, "Reduce the wanting – kill the greed." I repeated the quote to him to make sure I had heard it correctly, and then its meaning started to sink in. Each moment that passed, it sunk further and further into me, with memories of where I had not heeded that wisdom.

On my way out, I grabbed a simple piece of paper and wrote the quote down, folded it, and put in my pocket. It is the one quote that now sits on that same piece of paper on top of my desk at home as a constant reminder to myself of that wisdom. I used the quote as a gateway to the level where I am now - the level of total surrender.

The force of this fight is one that buckles your knees and snaps the blood and bones in them and then dares you to stand again if you want to continue to fight. It holds your life in its grasp. It thinks and knows it has the upper hand. This is what surrender means and what it takes to stand up. The look in my eyes does not come from me. It was within me, but I was keeping it away. The look comes from surrendering to my faith.

Wednesday night I just swung my legs over the side of my bed and then just sat there trying to summon everything I had to just stand. My body shook from the fight. It was all I could do to just swing my legs out of bed and just sit up, but I wanted to go for a walk. It is my goal twice each day. They tell me I need to walk, but rarely do I see anyone on this east floor walking. I glanced at the clock, and it was 8:50 PM When I glanced again, it was a quarter after nine. I had not moved. I now understood why people do not walk, but it is not always like this.

The intense roller coaster ride of this treatment plays on my physical and mental willpower. There are times I can move and act almost like my old self and

• • • •

then others where I can hardly just even move. The struggle continues to forge character and lasting change. The ride of this illness is raw with powerful lessons of love at its core.

This treatment has opened my eyes to what it feels like to suffer. We have all seen the harshness around the world these recent years on marriages, jobs, communities and much more. Caught in the middle have been children and innocent people. Let's pray that those who cause suffering will realize their wrongs and dedicate the rest of their days to doing what is right. I can help by starting with my life and all the people I touch. I need to stop contributing to that kind of suffering in the world. True suffering is harsh.

This disease knows no sympathy. It tries to find every weakness: physical, mental, spiritual. It will try to make you do unnatural things and break your character. But, that has been my strength. It is relentless but so am I. It keeps knocking me down, but I keep getting up. I keep walking and talking and smiling. If I give an inch, it will take a mile to get back.

When the nurse brings my pre-chemo medicines in the early morning, I just grab my rosary and pray my intentions. It may be for people I just met or a moment for you in your life that I remember. The door knocks and the chemo comes. I curl up and imagine Audrey coming into our bedroom at home. She comes in each day as our six-year-old alarm clock. She gets into bed with Kathryn and me. I sit up, and she crawls between me and my pillow. She sinks into the covers and giggles with delight. I hold and pull her in close. Each day is so precious and one day she will be too big to come in.

• • • •

Yesterday, the first thing Audrey did when she came for a visit was ask if she could climb on my hospital bed. Then she snuggled right in. Little did she know that as they drip, push, or inject my spine with chemo, it does not matter. I am just there holding my little Audrey in my thoughts of early morning dawn in our home. The only thing strong enough for this fight is my faith.

My faith serves as an endless supply of every need I have on this roller coaster ride. It is there with everything anytime I call. It is unwavering in its love and support. Faith was taught to me by my parents as it was from their parents to them. It is this passing down of life's important lessons that we give to our family. I am the youngest of six children. Family is my life. I am sustained by the immense love of my brothers and sisters. I cannot categorize my family into the normal delineations. My nieces and nephews I treat as my own. It is a beautiful example that my mother and father taught us. In a prior letter, I wrote about my great-great grandfather Anton, but I missed an important point. If I were able to talk to him, one of the most important things he would want to communicate to me is that love that he received from his wife.

Great-Great Grandmother Elizabeth, I am sure, had many great untold stories of her and the life she led. I will never know them. But, the one story I do know is that of my wife Kathryn. From the moment we first met, she truly has been endless joy for me. I have witnessed her impact on other lives with her unceasing focus on others. She has taught in preschool now for fifteen years, so when we walk around our St. Francis

• • • •

of Assisi community, it is like I am with the Pied-Piper, and children of all ages and their parents come forth to greet Ms. Kathryn.

When you say, "I do" at the altar, you are really not thinking that something like this would ever be real. But yet, here we find ourselves, facing one of life's biggest tests of all. I am in awe of her strength, and her ability to maintain normalcy for our children through this all. Kathryn's grandmother taught me to never judge others, not at all. I see Kathryn also doing this so well. I can only imagine the strength of those pioneers like our great-great grandparents, but in my wife, I see their example. She is the love of my life, the woman of my dreams, and the incredible mother of our children.

Kathryn has blessed me with Brock, Vince, Gretchen and Audrey who are endless sources of joy. Brock is a growing 6 foot 2 inch tower of integrity who is a role model of mine. Vince is not far behind and brings a gift of intelligence and warm tender heart that will make someone one day the luckiest girl ever. Gretchen exudes life and radiates beauty wherever she goes. She will never be a poker player, but her wonderful emotions connect with anyone at just the right time. Audrey is the sparkplug that never wears out. She can make you feel like first time parents by saying and doing the most amazing unexpected things. It gives me such peace to know they are in your hands now too.

I cannot begin to thank all of you enough for the many kinds of support you have given to Kathryn and our children, only some of which I know... so much of

• • • •

what you just do. So please understand my humble attempt to thank you.

I also see support from strangers, which are now becoming friends here in the hospital. I see health care at its best from the people who create it. I am seeing why people become nurses and doctors. I am seeing all the people who support them at their best. I do not see perfection. I do not expect perfection. It does not exist. There are so many variables and so many challenges. I am just grateful how hard they try. These doctors and nurses are amazing, but it is just as hard on them as it is on me to try to find the right way to treat a disease whose only goal is to conquer. I see others at their best. Principals and teachers watch over our children as their own. Boy Scouts, Knights, and neighbors there for any need. There are friends who just give and give and give.

My room is very simple, and I love it. I have a small Christmas tree with an angel on top from a friend, Nancy, which Kathryn decorated with our children's ornaments from long ago. You know the kind made with a kid's picture in the middle put together with scissors and paper, felt and glue. On the shelf there is a picture of my family and our dog Kenna at Bear Island one summer. Sitting on the shelf is a green duck with orange feet and a bright yellow beak - Kathryn's added touch to ensure I keep a smile on my face. Below there are two pictures of Kathryn & I back in college before we were married. One picture is of us and the other is of a heart drawn in cement with our initials KK & JJ. A crystal ABC block sits in front of the picture frame as a lasting and loving reminder of the three children we did not get to raise.

Another shelf has a bright red frame with smiley faces all over it. Enclosed in it is our six year-old Audrey's note to me given to me that one day in the ENT office, "To Dad, I hope it goes well!   Love, Audrey."

A solid block of marble sits on the shelf.   On its sides are engraved plates with the CHRIST Principles of Caring, Humility, Respect, and Integrity. On top is a circle with no beginning or end - with one word in the middle. The circle represents the last two principles of Sportsmanship and Teamwork. The inside of the circle that you cannot see represents the faith in ourselves, in each other, and in the one word in the center, which is "GOD."

Each week during the season, I asked the basketball team to focus on one of those words as our word of the week. The players were asked to share one example each day with their families of something they did that day to reflect that principle. At the end of the season, each player on the school's basketball team that I coached when Brock was in sixth grade was given this marble memento. It was meant to serve as a lasting reminder to them that as they go forward in life they can draw upon its meaning, its memories, and its principles for a solid foundation in life.

The last item in my room I just received from the current basketball team. I coached these players last year and through the past summer. Vince entitled the ball 'Life is Joyful', and written all around it were inspirational comments from each player.   The consistent word they all used was Kia Kaha. The word Kia Kaha came from one of my team movie nights, where we watched the film, *Forever Strong*.   It was a true story based on the life and coaching dedication of Larry Gelwix. He had a phenomenal sports record, but what is far more phenomenal about him is that he has created decades of players with Honor, Hard Work, Commitment, Sacrifice, Dedication, Family, Education, and Health that he taught in the building of their life long character.

Mother Teresa's main character trait was that of a 'doer.' From my reading of her, she never offered to help or waited to be asked... She just did it. She saw a need and then worked to fulfill that need. She was one of the greatest people ever to lead by example through her deeds not her words. Because of such, when she did speak, her words were deep, powerful, and truthful.

I kidded with Kathryn the other night as we were lying in my bed holding each other. I said, "This would make a pretty good movie, wouldn't it? Our lives have been parts of all of our favorite movies: *Love Story, Facing the Giants, Rudy, Brian's Song, Cheaper by the Dozen, It's a Wonderful Life* and many more." We laughed. I said, "Unfortunately, Katherine Hepburn would not be able to play you anymore..." We laughed even harder when I asked who would play me. It would be a good movie though. From my eyes, I am seeing the world and people at their best. The title, of course, would be *Joy of Life*.

My Christmas gift to you is this letter. It is all that I have and that I am capable of giving now. My hope is that there can be a thought or two in my letters that will help you in some way and that you can fully embrace those you are lucky enough to be around on any given day. This is how our lives intersect with Mother Teresa, John Wooden, Coach Gelwix, you and me. We find goodness, examples, strength and in turn give back to each other.

One night while out for my night walk this week on the 2nd floor, which is nearly always empty, there were four people. As I began my back hallway run, I came upon these four people walking behind one another in a straight line with 5 to 6 feet between them. Their steps were heavy having just emerged from the ICU. The stride and strength of their walk resembled that of honest, hardworking, and putting others first family farmers. I had seen this strength of walk many times from my days in Iowa where my mom's family of 12 farmed the land. It looked like they knew they had to leave to get back to the farm where the ICU did not matter and needs had to be met.

I caught up with the family and stood next to the mom. I reached out my hand and put it gently on her back. She smiled at me, and I smiled at her. I said, "Cold out there." She replied, "Yes, very cold." As I stepped further ahead, I turned and said, "Stay warm and have a good night." She smiled again and said, "Thank you." She trudged on in that same line toward the door. We had connected and nothing more needed to be said. I in my hospital gown and IV pole in hand, and she with her son or her daughter or her family/friend member left behind. These are good decent, hardworking people trying to summon the energy needed to put one foot in front of another. I saw my great-great grandfather and grandmother in this family knowing they had made that same walk three times.

To my friends who practice their Shinto, Jewish, Hindu, Islamic, Buddhist, Atheism, and the rainbow of

• • • •

many Christian faiths, I wish you in my Catholic faith a Merry Christmas. May it bring you much joy and (at the soul of this Christmas greeting) love. Thank you for all the acts of kindness and love to our family. Kathryn and I are so humble. Please know we are well cared for.

God has just given me the best Christmas present I have ever received. He is letting me unwrap the CHRIST within. For me, that is the true gift of Christmas. Rediscovering the CHRIST within ourselves... Bringing it forth in daily life through our words and in our actions.

I believe in the good in people. I am an optimist. I believe there are no bad children only ones who need the right role model and someone that believes in what they are capable of. I believe each of us makes a difference. Each day. In everything we do. How we greet strangers. How we look for opportunities to help. I like to make someone just smile by finding a way to connect. It could be as simple as commenting on their fun shirt or their cool shoes. But it can be looking a little deeper and reading their face for an opportunity to make a difference in their day.

You have done that for me with your friendship. I have witnessed you doing immeasurable examples of kindness, love, friendship, and fun. You maybe did not know I was watching or saw what you did, but I did. I learned from you and added to myself. I put a part of you in me. That piece of goodness to save to give out at the right opportunity.

For the first time in my life, I understand suffering. The burning in my mouth reminds me to use my words to give others joy. Instead of causing suffering, I can help heal.

There is a harsh reality around me. One of my neighbors, a patient on the floor, passed away this morning. We had not met yet to become friends, and I am still waiting to hear his name. His will be on top of my prayer list with a tear as to "why?"

Today they are filling me with three liquids and the chemo of which will run all day. Soon, unfortunately, I will be ordered to wear a mask to protect my health when I walk outside my room. Some people may not see me in the same way, but know that I will be smiling no matter what.

Last year, Kathryn gave me the best Christmas present she has ever given me - four black and white 8x10 wooden framed photos of our children. She captured their joy in her photos, and I can look at them for hours.

Twenty-seven of the last twenty-eight years Kathryn and I have left at this time for her grandmother's house. If there is a heaven on earth for Kathryn, it is found in her grandmother's home sitting in the kitchen talking, laughing, and baking. My heart just breaks that she cannot be there now. Grandma fell this year and is under care in a rehabilitation facility. The house is being sold, but the love and memories will always remain.

Kathryn's mother passed away from a long battle with lupus when she was just four months old. Her grandmother raised Kathryn for those first few years as her Dad tried to regroup from the loss of his high

• • • •

school sweetheart. Reflecting now, I remember holding Kathryn in her grandmother's house our first Christmas together when we were dating. I felt very lucky. That feeling is still there but has grown stronger and now holds strong love for our children, my family and you, my friends.

I won't kid you this pain is raw, and it is real. Every day nurses ask multiple times, "What is your pain level?" They ask me to give them a number for my pain on a scale from 0-10. The scale on the door is a series of bright yellow smiley faces ultimately decreasing into a frown. Each face has corresponding numbers so it can be used with kids and adults. I deeply appreciate their concern and question each time. They now smile with me when I smile and give them my same response, "No complaints".

Wednesday was my toughest day so far. At the end of this day, however, I was given an amazing gift. Kathryn had returned home to put our children to bed. My youngest sister was reading to me, and my middle brother had just called. I could not read or watch TV. I could not really talk as my mouth was so sore. I just handed the phone to Joan to give an update when I heard singing coming from the halls.

Christmas carolers. They had come in on a cold 25 degree night here in Raleigh to bring their warmth of a song to my fellow patients and me. I did not want to move. I had just handed the phone to my sister to talk for me, and yet I knew I needed to get out of bed to open the door and thank them. They were just about to leave when I opened my door, smiled, and said, "Thanks for your wonderful gift. Know how grateful we are."

• • • •

They smiled, and one said," Well, do you have a favorite song we could sing for you?" I said, "No, please pick any." I then sat on a chair in the hall. I sat and waited for the song to begin. She simply said, "OK then. How about this one?" They broke into "Joy to the World!"

Jerome

Christmas Update
(A note from Kathryn)
Monday, December 27, 2010, 8:00 PM

We hope you all had a great Christmas with your loved friends and family. Our Christmas Day was filled with joy! The nursing staff at Rex provided our room with blankets, and we all celebrated together in an old fashioned way-sitting on the floor taking turns opening gifts to one another. The kids and I also went to Joan and Jacques' house in the afternoon to celebrate with cousins and Jerome's mom.

When we drove home, we were thrilled with a beautiful snowfall! At our house, we measured eight inches! It was white, heavy, crisp, and provided delayed transportation everywhere! The snow stuck to the limbs of the trees and was gorgeous. Someone said that it had not snowed on Christmas for 60 some years! We were grateful for our kind neighbors who chipped in (literally) to shovel snow off our driveway on Sunday so we could get the car in the garage! I guess Wisconsin came to us this year!

• • • •

Since Jerome's last update, he has ridden the rollercoaster ride up and down. He is making progress in the right direction in spite of the many challenges the intensive chemo provides. He had low hemoglobin, and he received two pints of blood, which helped. His white blood cell count is extremely low, so the nurses and doctors continue to monitor. His mouth has been very sore, so yesterday they started to give him all nutrition by IV... no more food by mouth! I'm freezing all those goodies at home (especially the cookies).

Jerome's immune system is nonexistent right now. Please understand that he cannot have visitors outside of the family at this time. He needs to rest and get strong. The doctors are altering his treatment plan daily and are discussing when and how they want to proceed with the second cycle of treatment. We are open to their plan. Jerome has his GI doctor on board to help with some abdominal challenges. Dr. Schwarz has guided Jerome through many challenges for the past fifteen years and has become a great resource and friend to have on Jerome's healthcare team.

Daily walks in the halls continue. In fact I came to visit today and Jerome was off walking with his sister, Joan! I traveled the usual path route (to the 2nd floor nursery, over the 'bridge', and past the chapel). I thought it was odd that the door was closed, but walked by thinking that perhaps someone was having a service or prayer. Later I found out that they were in the chapel and had closed the door! Audrey and I stopped in tonight to go for another walk with Jerome.

Jerome now resembles Kojak (minus the Tootsie Pop). I gave him a "0" haircut yesterday. I think he looks very handsome. I miss the grey hair and the

● ● ● ●

beard, but since it was leaving on its own accord, we thought best to get rid of it quicker than not! Well, the team is ready to roll... Again, we so appreciate all the prayers and support from each of you. We are getting through this because of all of you!

Be kind to yourself today!

Love and Peace,
Kathryn

Happy New Year
(A note from Kathryn)
Sunday, January 2, 2011, 8:00 PM

Happy New Year to all of you! We cannot even begin to thank everyone for the many ways in which you have touched our family over the past several months. I am not able to write an individual note to each of you like I would like. That bothers me. Please know we have been and still are enjoying all the fun things and delicious dinners that have come our way. Your prayers and support continue to uplift us each day.

We had an unexpected surprise on Friday (New Year's Eve)... Jerome's levels allowed him to come home! He has been doing a lot of sleeping☺, and he looks fantastic! The kids were thrilled to see him home. Audrey got some snuggle time in. Gretchen and Jerome got to watch some "Seventh Heaven" episodes. Brock got to work on college applications with Dad, once again, and Vince was glued to the television with

Jerome to watch the Packers play. Jerome even ate real food!

Luzann (Jerome's sister) came to Raleigh from Boston on Wednesday to help out. She helped me pack up our entire Christmas decor yesterday. She was a blessing! We had a great visit with her and Jerome's other sister Joan and her family. Today we gathered to watch the Packer-Bear Game with Granny Lou. Now you haven't watched a Packer game until you see Granny Lou (at age 96) cheering and hollering for a turnover! Whew! Now there was a great start to the New Year!

This morning we were able to go to St. Francis for Mass. This was a highlight for Jerome... Both boys were altar serving, Jerome's mom and sister joined us, and it was a beautiful Mass. We looked around the church and it was though we were seeing St. Francis Parish for the first time through a new set of lenses. Jerome especially felt like he had truly come home to his family.

We plan to meet with Dr. Yoffe on Tuesday morning to discuss Cycle #2 and our next course of action. We are anticipating re-entry to Rex on Tuesday or Wednesday. Give a great Packer hug to someone you love! Peace and good things to you all!

Love,
Kathryn

• • • •

Cycle #2 Almost Done!

(A note from Kathryn)
Saturday, January 8, 2011, 4:00 PM

Wow! We are now into Cycle #2 already. The fabulous nursing staff wasted no time in administering Jerome's pre-chemo treatment, and soon Jerome was receiving his first of three chemo drugs, which will become his regular daily routine. The moment we walked into his new room, the food service delivery man remembered Jerome and asked asked if he ordered a serving of macaroni and cheese. Jerome said, "No, I haven't had the chance to order yet. We just arrived." They laughed and agreed to leave it for a tasty treat.

This cycle of treatment is going well so far for Jerome. He came in on Wednesday after getting the doctor to agree to a Wednesday vs. Tuesday admission to give him 4 1/2 days at home. Although his body is physically much more worn out, he is spiritually and mentally growing much stronger. The time with the kids and being home really renewed him and his spirits. He had good reports from the doctors, and they along with the nurses do such a wonderful job responding as soon as challenges come up so quickly with this intense treatment.

Jerome will continue the conclusion of this cycle of chemo treatment with his fourth spinal infusion on Monday. Then he will come home for about 2-3 weeks with visits to the Cancer Center along the way to check levels. He will return to Rex for the 3rd cycle of treatment (repeating the Cycle 1 chemo drugs), and he will be in the hospital for 3-4 weeks during that time.

● ● ● ●

After he returns home he will be monitored for a couple more weeks, then have a PET and CT scan to evaluate the results of the chemo. He will continue to have annual evaluations to make sure the lymphoma has not returned. He will head into the colon cancer surgery sometime in the spring when he is physically strong enough for the two surgeries.

Jerome has had a few lingering challenges overall with the chemo treatment. One of the longest and painful side effects has been the skin peeling off his fingertips of his first three fingers on each hand. New skin has grown in but is super sensitive to touch. He is unable to do basic things. He has some neuropathy in his left two fingers and toes in his feet.

It is great to see how the kids have all rallied to pitch in to help Jerome while he was home. Brock helped with buttoning Jerome's shirts, putting on and taking off shirts, Gretchen helped with opening containers and carrying things, Vince ran around the house getting whatever Jerome needed, and even Audrey brought her stuffed giraffe Jaffy into bed to snuggle with Jerome. It was cute as she woke him out of a dead sleep to check with him to see if he wanted to use her coveted stuffed animal to snuggle with. Jerome said yes to her offer and she very happily scampered away to retrieve Jaffy for Jerome.

The kids have learned a lot about giving from this experience. We see them growing so much stronger as they see first-hand the strong physical changes with their dad losing weight, losing hair, and losing physical strength. Much strength comes from the tremendous support from you, our family, and Jerome's calming presence. We have also been very careful to try to

• • • •

keep all their routines. It has worked really well. We are so deeply grateful to so many of you for helping make this happen.

Jerome had a very touching moment yesterday when he entered the small chapel in the hospital and found three people gathered in the front pew. He gently asked, "And who are we praying for today?" as all three arose when he entered. He could see one woman was very distressed. She replied, "My husband." She shared the diagnosis with him as he reached her. He said he softly put his hand on her shoulder and shared some thoughts with her and then told her that God does not make mistakes. He said at that point she fell into his arms and cried into his shoulder repeating over and over these words, "God does not make mistakes." He told her that he loved her and kissed her through his mask on her forehead. Jerome told her that he would pray for her husband.

Jerome said he saw her outside of the critical cardiac care unit on his walk today. She told him that her husband had talked to her and was making some progress. She said he still has a long ways to go, but she was so grateful. They repeated together again that God does not make mistakes. She hugged him and said, "I am praying for you too."

This is an example of the types of blessings that Jerome has experienced several times each day since his journey began. It has energized him. He feels God's hand is all over all of us. We have been so humbled. You all have been such a blessing with your words and actions. Thank you! The pictures I mentioned have now been posted and hopefully many of them will make you

• • • •

smile. We are doing well and feeling your love. Thank you for your prayers and know you are in ours too.

Love,
Kathryn

Round Three
(A note from Kathryn)
Sunday, January 23, 2011, 9:45 PM

Hello to each of you!

Wow! What a difference a week can make. This past week we continued to see first-hand the severe roller coaster ride the doctor told us we might experience. Jerome came home eleven days ago and was feeling pretty good. The doctors wanted to get him out of the hospital before his levels hit bottom (to help avoid catching any serious infection). Dr. Yoffe warned that Jerome might hit bottom in a few days. Jerome went into the Cancer Center to get his final chemo drugs Friday to check his blood levels. His white cell count did not register a reading; his neutrophil count (which measures his ability to fight infection) was 0.00. His hemoglobin and platelet levels were falling fast. Friday night brought the major change, and he was suddenly incapacitated with nausea and pain. He spent 95% of the weekend in bed and could barely move.

Jerome was really hurting on Saturday. He was only able to watch the 1st quarter of the Packer playoff game with us before going. He was not able to eat much of anything, but we all smiled a bit on Sunday

• • • •

night when Jerome requested Brock drive up to the store for a box of Sugar Pops! He successfully ate three bowls! After the weekend and an entire box of Sugar Pops (he even hid them from the kids!), Jerome started to get stronger. I think Kellogg's might want to use Jerome for a commercial?! This past Wednesday he met with Dr. Yoffe and was surprised that he would be going back into the hospital on Monday, January 24th. We thought he had another week at home, but by tomorrow his platelets should be at the minimum level needed to put him back in the hospital for Round Three of the chemo.

Going back into the hospital this time is a bit more challenging for Jerome. The first time Jerome went into the hospital, he felt his experience was like walking on a railroad track and getting hit by a series of freight trains. He did not know when the train was coming, what side effects the drugs would bring, or how hard the side effects would hit. Round Three of the chemo will be a repeat of Round One.

Now Jerome feels like he is walking on the train tracks and heading directly into the freight trains with his eyes wide open. He knows what is coming. He said it is a much different mental preparation. Jerome shared that insight with his doctor and said he really needed until Monday to get mentally and physically ready to proceed with Round Three. Dr. Yoffe understood and shared with Jerome that he too had to mentally prepare to give Jerome the last three spinals. That meant so much to Jerome. Jerome could really feel how hard it is on the doctors to put their patients through this severe chemotherapy treatment and its effects.

• • • •

I know this website was set up for Jerome's news, but on Thursday this past week, I stepped just the wrong way on a curbed sidewalk and dove headfirst into the cement. I was not able to break my fall. Needless to say, I was very fortunate to have walked away with only a large abrasion, a puck-sized swollen forehead, and to date, one very purple eye-shadowed gothic style black right eye. The left eye is starting to turn colors as I am writing this note! Never a dull moment here! Thanks for the quick response of the people who were there with quick and kind offers of ice and help. Guess I was just feeling a little left out?! I can certainly say without any doubt that Jerome looks a lot better than I do right now!

Jerome had a much better weekend. He was re-energized a bit by going to St. Francis for Mass and a couple of the kids' events. It was good to feel a little normalcy again. Although physically it will be tough to dive into Round Three tomorrow, Jerome is mentally ready. I think the Packers win today and heading to the Super Bowl helped too☺.

We continue to be blessed with so many kind thoughts, actions, and food from all of you. Please know how much your presence in our lives strengthens our spirit. Thank you for your continued prayers and support.

Peace,
Kathryn

This Week with the Friedmans
(A note from Kathryn)
Sunday, January 30, 2011, 8:45 PM

What a beautiful day! The temperature was in the mid 50's and the sunshine was glorious. Jerome was commenting on the unbelievable sunrise he saw out his window this morning. The kids and I went up to the hospital after church this morning. Jerome looked great, and he felt fairly well. His fingers are starting to peel. His mouth continues to be extremely dry and sore. The Biotene seems to really help. Overall, he has experienced more nausea this time around than before. Today he had 'off' from the chemo, so we all enjoyed the break.

We were able to take a nice walk with Kenna (our dog) around the parking lots at Rex for about forty minutes. It was wonderful to spend time with Jerome outside and soak up some warmth in body and in spirit. Kenna really has missed her walking buddy, so she really enjoyed walking along the side of Jerome and his IV pole! Jerome's machine started beeping and our time came to a close, but I promise next time I will bring a camera to take a picture or two to post up on the website! I am certain the Rex Hospital staff thought we were 'breaking out' as we passed the front desk!

Jerome will have his last Lumbar Puncture on Friday. He will continue to have Methotrexate for 24 hours and then Leucovorin every 6 hours for 72 hours after the methotrexate is done. Of course, any of this can change according to how he responds to treatment. We are getting closer to the end of our time at Rex! We cross a day at a time off the calendar at home. Jerome was in the hospital for 23 days for the

• • • •

first cycle. We are focused on Sunday and the Super Bowl. Jerome's GI doctor, "Coach" has already reserved his seat in the hospital family room with Jerome for the big game! We are very excited for the Packers and the state of Wisconsin!

Thank you to all those who have provided us with the delicious food, special services (my car looks the best ever!), and help with the kids. A special shout out goes out to Ashley at St. Francis who let Gretchen borrow her shoes for basketball practice on Monday night. I have heard of giving the shirt off your back... but she gave the shoes off her feet! I could not get to practice because I took a trip to the ER for a CT scan on my face. All turned out fine, but the five hour wait at WakeMed North allowed me some special opportunities. I enjoyed watching the Australian Open and The Oprah Winfrey Show. Just spending that amount of time in a quiet room was a gift!

One of my three-year old students kept staring at me this week saying, "That doesn't look right!" My skin is now green and gold in the spirit of the game! One might think that I planned this?! The preschool will be celebrating the Super Bowl on Thursday and Friday this week. We will be making cheeseheads and participating in tailgating parties! Go Pack Go!

I hope you all have a great week!

Peace,
Kathryn and crew

Prayer & Reflections

(A note from Jerome)
Sunday, February 6, 2011, 3:15 AM

Dear Family & Friends,

Please join me in offering up your prayers for two families next door to me at Rex who have been coming to the hospital to spend time with loved ones. Their loved one's struggles with cancer have now ended. One was an older mother who passed away next to me in the middle of the night. The other was a younger man across the hall who passed away late yesterday. Both had really suffered in recent months and days. I heard their screams from cancer's cruel pains that never ceased in spreading to so many parts of their bodies. The mother was an example of an older parent who lived a full life in the loving care of her family. It is never easy to see a parent go. Loving them and wanting more time with them is a testament to the beautiful, endless bond between parent and child.

The man's death was especially difficult because he was a young father saying goodbye to several young children. They needed more time together. I heard one of his children suddenly crying out without warning yesterday the moment after he passed away bringing a gripping freeze to my life. It endlessly flowed into my room from the hall. Inconsolable sobbing sounds that brought with it a rawness and hurting tenderness that knew no depth. Sounds I will never forget. The deep cries came from a loving pain escaping from a child's heart unable to deal with the absence of a dad. I could feel those penetrating sounds over and over resonating with pain - A child's love crying and reaching out for comfort from anyone. The cry brought a desperate

••••

longing desire for a future with a father that would never be.

It is difficult to describe my feelings building from the past several days. I would step out of my room and see this flow of families and friends that kept coming. I thought it was just for visits to a sick family member or friend, which is a normal part of the day here. This floor houses those who are so desperately ill with the harshest and/or deadliest of cancers.

I learned that these were people coming in to say last words. I saw so much in their eyes. They told many stories from so many memories. They would gather both in small and large groups. There was laughter thankfully too, but also so many whispered conversations, or just standing around with blank stares or private cell phone calls leaning against walls. They were here early. They were here late. When you studied them closer, the different body languages all communicated the same message. They were all facing a life fact that time was quickly ending. They came to just touch, talk, and visit the one they loved. This was another vivid reality of my hospital home here on 5 East. Life and death are literally right next door to me and can appear at any moment as each day unfolds. It snaps you into the reality of the gift of gratefulness for every moment of every day. It also lets you be honored, truly honored, to see nurses and doctors who try so hard to defeat cancer.

I have been blessed with all the doctors and nurses from all medical professions who have cared for me so well. It is unfair to them for all their life saving efforts when these cancers or other diseases are successful with cruel distorted goals. What goes through their

• • • •

minds when this happens despite their exhausting efforts? Each patient they lose along the way rips out a part of their hearts. They lovingly ease the patient into God's arms in those final days and then must summon the strength to continue on as other patients' needs call.

Multiple times each day I go down to the 2nd floor nursery and look through the windows at the new life that has arrived that day. I just love it! It is the most beautiful part of my day seeing the newly born babies and sometimes being lucky enough to talk and share the joy with new parents, grandparents or friends gathered at the windows of life. I pray for each of those new lives and the beautiful innocence coming into this world. I pray to God that their lives will have strong value based guidance that will be lasting and true for them as their lives will be shaped from so many angles by the daily life we provide in our world. It is so clear to me that we really do join their lives in so many tangible and intangible ways by serving as mentors teaching them by how we live our lives in this world. How we love and care for one another as Christ has taught us. We are responsible as women and men of our rainbow of beautiful faiths around this world. I pray that they may always keep the one quality and fact that is so evident in the nursery... the incredible joy that life brings and how each child starts with the same beating human heart.

Thank you for your prayers. Love and peace to you and your families. Really savor life and the lives of tomorrow which will be brought into each day. Death may bring tears of reminders and longing for what might have been, but then we must return to the joy of life every day by laughing, singing, and enjoying the

• • • •

gifts of this amazing life around us. It is so important how we live that next day.

Help make those around you smile each day with the gift of yourself. We all know ways to make a baby smile... smiles really are contagious. This is so important. This is what John Wooden meant when he strongly quoted and mentored to me Mother Teresa's words, "Unless a life is lived for others, it is not worthwhile." Those are powerful words that hit me right between the eyes asking me if I am living my life just for myself. It told me we have to be active mentors to those around us each day with how we live. The words we choose. The actions we take. We all can be so quick to criticize or judge those around us. It is easy to do and a sin we are all guilty of too frequently. But, that is not what God is asking us. And, judging others is His job and His only.

God is asking us to use His son's incredible examples to live our lives. That is the role model He gave us. Our role is to love those around us. Help those around us. Encourage, care and nurture those around us.

I admire my wife Kathryn's grandmother's wisdom and her incredible example. I have witnessed over 28 years of her loving kindness always welcoming all into her home. I rarely have ever heard Grandma in all those years criticize or judge anyone. Did she have reason to? Could she have been bitter with God or feel she had been wronged in life? Yes.

God took three of Grandma's seven children from her way too soon. Her first loss was Kathryn's mother Gretchen. She died from lupus four months after

••••
117

giving birth to Kathryn. Gretchen and her young husband Bob were just starting their married lives together. Suddenly Grandma and Bob were dealt the toughest of body blows knocking both of them into a blowing wind of mourning for years to come.

Seven years later, God took Grandma's young daughter, Nancy. She was a loving mother to little Cari and was pregnant with her second child - a little boy. Nancy died from acute leukemia within weeks of her diagnosis. Her baby did not survive. Nancy's beloved husband Don felt such a loss that he never married another.

Henry died in 2009. Grandma told me this was her most difficult loss. Her response surprised me. Why was the loss of one child harder than another? How could one compare losses of multiple children? How could one even go there? She explained so I could understand. She gave birth to Henry 73 years earlier. Henry had been with her longer than anyone else on face of this earth including her deceased husband Oscar. Henry attended to her every need. Only twenty minutes away, he had always been there for her. Always. Grandma lost her firstborn son to pancreatic cancer. It was quick, without warning, and so unfair.

Why and how does Grandma show no lasting bitterness, no real criticism, and no passing judgment of others? Because hers is the purest love born, grown and given freely from within her soul to others. It comes from a lifetime of love, study, gratefulness, reflection and daily prayers given to her from teachings of Christ. She has answers provided to her from an unwavering faithfulness to God.

● ● ● ●

Kathryn is my living role model. I see her trying to live out each day by honoring her grandmother's strong powerful lessons taught by example. Kathryn just gives and gives and gives to those around her. She has not only lovingly mentored our children with these teachings but also for over 15 years she has mentored new classes of preschoolers at St. Francis. She has taught them with wonderful laughter, fun and fullness. She loves her work so much. How else can you explain a mother who takes a break from her own family of four to serve a classroom full of three-years-olds day after day? That is pure love and genuine desire to serve.

Why must we all be active mentors to serve? My answer to this question is what Mother Teresa's example teaches us. I am learning not to ask. It takes their time, energy and efforts to tell you what and when. Rather, it is so much more powerful and beneficial to just look for the opportunities to help. If we truly aspire to help as Mother Teresa did, we do it by how she lived... she opened her loving eyes for opportunities to help make a difference. When she saw a need she acted without the delay of a question. She did it with a joy and fullness of love in her heart that mirrored the one she prayed to every day for strength and guidance to continue her work.

This is the strength that I am building into my character to make this world a better place. I am learning to be self-disciplined to ultimately stop criticism and judgment of others. It is of no benefit to judge others who act differently than how we think they should act. Even worse is commenting to others about these useless and unhelpful thoughts and shortcomings we perceive.

• • • •

I try to focus and hold myself accountable on how I am thinking and acting which is fully and always in my control. Each day I ask myself if I am bringing benefit to others around me in my words and actions. Why must we all stop and do better on this? Because just maybe, just maybe, that person we are criticizing, just maybe that person's behavior we are crossing over to judge for God, just maybe that person might be someone like the little boy down the hall whose piercing sobs went straight into my heart and soul. What that little boy needs are people throughout his life to be caring role models in the absence of his dad.

There are so many people who just need others around them in life to care. Everyone in this world can benefit with how we simply live our lives and share our thoughts with each other each day. Opportunities are all around us to make a difference. It does not have to take losing a parent to have a need for this mentoring help.

Our world is tough enough and filled with so many challenges thrown at all of us. We just need to realize that each day we are given a choice in how to live. We choose the words that come out of our mouths and the actions we use when no one is watching. We have control. We all have the incredible gift and power to bring forth the commitment to be a living example and a powerful mentor to those we touch each day.

Jerome

Super Fun Green Bay Packer Surprise
(A note from Kathryn)
Tuesday, February 8, 2011, 9:30 PM

Peace and all good things to you! What a week, and it is only Tuesday! Sunday's game was a definite highlight and distraction for Jerome! We were both concerned on Sunday morning though, when his television did not work! No one seemed to understand the importance of this dilemma except perhaps the other Green Bay fans! By game time he still did not have TV, so we moved next door to watch the game with sound! "Coach" Dr. Schwarz joined us for the first half of the game, and we were thrilled to share some Wisconsin tailgating spirit with him. I regret not having a camera for pictures of that team-building moment. It was special. The tone was set for the game.

I (Kathryn) only had to apologize for my enthusiasm once when the door was left open. In fact, after the game one of the nurses commented to Jerome that he had more fun watching my excitement than the game! Jerome's sister Joan was holding down the fort back home with our kids, Sarah, and Will. Joan admitted she watched the fourth quarter through her covered eyes! Granny Lou cheered on the Packers at the house too. She was the Packers' secret weapon!

Monday brought "The Day After" phenomenon. Those in Wisconsin know what I'm talking about. The feeling of the day is determined by the outcome of the day before... and what a GREAT Monday it was! Jerome carried that feeling into a tremendously challenging day. More on that later. Dr. Yoffe surprised him with 2 new Packers shirts to celebrate the win. It helped carry

••••

him through the LP and the side effects, which were the worst yet.

Today I came home from work and found a large box on our front steps from the Green Bay Packers Office! Big "G" tape surrounded the box. We took it to the hospital. There was the BIG surprise! Jerome's nurse today (Katherine) was from Wisconsin, so we had her come in for the Grand Opening! The show stealer was a personalized note to Jerome signed by Aaron Rodgers! The package also contained a wonderful fleece Green Bay blanket, key chain, pen, and book highlighting the Packers and Green Bay. There was an autographed 8x10 picture of Aaron Rodgers too! It was amazing! Whoever the angel was out there that is responsible for that happening, I thank you so much! Jerome was so surprised! Again, he tolerated today a little better because of that kindness shared (The boys and the family are in awe of this as well!).

The pictures on the site show Jerome's room. I wish I would've had my camera at the hospital for the actual game. As it was I missed the Star Spangled Banner (maybe that was a good thing?!). I would have really liked a picture of Dr. Schwarz, Jerome, and myself enjoying the first half of the game together. Our memories are priceless.

Monday was the last lumbar chemo puncture injection. It came with a series of side effects that have hit Jerome all at once from different angles with gripping physical pains leaving him incapacitated for 5 to 10 minutes a couple times a day. The great news though is Jerome's spirits have never been stronger mentally or spiritually. He has no complaints.

• • • •

Before this last round of chemo, Jerome felt a strong nudge to watch the *The Passion of the Christ* with Brock and Vince. Now he knows why. The scourging at the pillar scene when Christ's clenched fists and arms shake uncontrollably as he rises again to his feet after the first forty lashes is what Jerome's arms and fists do when he is in pain. Jerome does not share this with you for you to feel sorry for him, but wanted you to know how blessed he feels to have experienced intense moments of suffering. The searing intensity of the pain has connected him directly to the cross. Jerome is grateful that God has allowed him the experience to further connect with his faith. He told me last night that this is the most powerful connection in his life.

Thank you again for all your prayers, food, kindness, and support (especially all the help with the kids this week).

Your journey with us makes us ONE.

Love in Christ,
Kathryn

Specific Prayer Request
(A note from Kathryn)
Sunday, February 13, 2011, 8:45 PM

Dear Friends,

This weekend has been a very rough one for Jerome. This note will be short because I have little time. Jerome has had fever for the last several days. Today his fever reached 104 degrees. He has pneumonia. Yesterday he received a blood transfusion, and today a platelet transfusion, so we hope these help. His white blood count and platelet count are extremely low. He really wanted to go out for a walk today, but was in no condition to go beyond the bathroom. He needed much encouragement to stay in the room☺.

Jerome is on heavy antibiotics. The chemo finished last Monday, but the mucositis is terrible. It is very painful. His legs and feet are quite swollen. He is being very courageous throughout this process. The medications have made it difficult for him to get any kind of quality sleep. Without the sleep he has had a very difficult time communicating clearly. Yesterday he told the kids that he had spent the day cleaning the house... Gretchen turned to me and said, "Is he making this stuff up?" I just smiled and said that I was glad that someone had cleaned the house, so I didn't have to spend the afternoon doing just that!

A huge thank you goes out to Jerome's sister Joan. She has spent endless hours with Jerome in his room and accompanied him on many walks over the last few weeks (especially this weekend) so I could be with the kids.

••••

To each of you who continue to pray, listen, cart kids around, watch our kids, feed us, and just smile when we pass by... We continue to say, Thank you and God Bless You all!

Please keep Jerome in your prayers that he will get through this stage of the treatment plan quickly and successfully. Pray the fever goes down, the pneumonia subsides, the mucositis heals, and all blood levels return to normal! I hope that isn't asking too much.

Much love,
Kathryn

A Note from Kathryn
Friday, February 18, 2011, 4:15 PM

Kathryn is off this weekend to Vince's basketball tournament, but she wanted to post an update for everyone.

Thank you for this week's prayer response. Jerome is making some positive gains in spite of the incredible challenges this week! His body is responding to the antibiotics and the fever is gone. He is down to 2 IVs at this time! Last night, he was able to get some much needed sleep. As I know, that makes everything clearer! His legs, knees, and feet are terribly swollen and painful. Our challenge is keeping his feet elevated. The mucositis is MUCH improved. He likes to keep up with his mouth care! He also enjoys his long, hot showers! (Some things never change☺!) Jerome is drinking as much as he can tolerate and we hope we

• • • •

can graduate to some solid foods soon. Jerome's stomach is distended, but we are told that when he returns to a regular diet, that will improve. We are grateful that the CT scans of his head were normal and that the infection in his lungs has not spread to the central nervous system.

It has been a difficult road. Each day gets better! Thank you for all you are doing for us and for all your prayers.

Love and good things to you all,
Kathryn

Jerome is home!

(A note from Kathryn)
Wednesday, February 23, 2011, 7:30 PM

I wanted to let you all know that Jerome came home from the hospital this afternoon. He is exhausted in body and re-energized in spirit! We are thrilled to have him back where he belongs for the recovery and prep for the next chapter of his life journey. We are so very grateful for all your continued prayers and support. This third cycle of treatment was extremely difficult. You have been Christ for us in our daily lives. You have lifted us up.

Thank you!
Kathryn

• • • •

Update at Home
(A note from Kathryn)
Thursday, March 3, 2011, 9:00 PM

Family and Friends,

It is nice to be communicating as a team again! We have survived a week back home together... Jerome has adapted pretty well to all my new household routines and rules☺!

Although it has been great having Jerome back home, his body is terribly worn-out from the chemo, pneumonia, fevers, and swelling. He is facing many daily challenges.

(1)His body is extremely weak. Every little movement throughout the day requires great effort and energy. He walks a little more each day. We are very grateful for the nice weather here and have walked to the park a few times with Kenna. She is happy Jerome is home too.

(2)Jerome continues to have intestinal cramps and flare ups that are wearing him down. This is one of his biggest challenges right now.

(3) His appetite is improving. Jerome is eating more of a normal diet now, and he is enjoying all the delicious food many of you have shared with us (I have stored much in the freezer)!

(4) Jerome is mentally exhausted. The treatment and fevers really took a toll on his concentration. He needs lots of rest.

● ● ● ●

We went to the oncologist yesterday to pose our questions and to get a report on Jerome's current condition. Dr. Yoffe was very pleased with how Jerome looked. We understand from the examination that the next 2-3 months will be a body building time for Jerome to heal and gain strength to get ready for the colon surgery. It is a long uphill battle. Next week we will have an appointment to re-check the status of Jerome's lungs/pneumonia. In four weeks Jerome will have the CT scan to determine if the chemo was successful.

As we venture forward, please continue to pray for continued physical and mental strength for Jerome. Pray that he can overcome his current health challenges, and that his lungs stay clear.

We are very grateful for all of the prayers and support (and food!) that you all have shared with us over the past several months. Thank you. We are overwhelmed by your friendship and presence in our lives.

Love,
Kathryn and Jerome

Spring Weather Brings Great Joy!
(A note from Kathryn)
Thursday, March 24, 2011, 3:15 PM

Your prayers and outpouring of support have been incredible! So many of you have been emailing and asking about how Jerome is doing. I wanted to get a

• • • •

quick note out to let you know how much we are enjoying Jerome at home. He is making small steps in the right direction!

Last week we met with the oncologist, Dr. Yoffe, for a check-up. Jerome's lungs have improved and are almost clear. He has about a week left on the antibiotics for the pneumonia. He just finished the treatment for the C diff and had positive final results. There were no new lumps that were found (Yeah!). The next step is the PET scan which will be done in the hospital in about three to four more weeks to find out whether or not the lymphoma is truly gone. We are hopeful. We are taking a day at a time and gaining strength for the upcoming colon surgery. Once the PET scan results for the lymphoma are in, we will meet with doctors to discuss the results and the colon cancer 'plan.'

Jerome is enjoying the warm weather and is able to get out for a daily walk to the park and back! He still has pain, but is pushing through it to gain leg and overall strength. His hair is starting to reappear in a little white stubble on the top of his head. He even has started to shave a little bit - Audrey and I insisted☺. Audrey brightens each morning for Jerome as she comes in with her morning wake up entrance and cuddle time with us.

Jerome has stepped up to the plate and tackled a few of the daily chores on our chore chart hanging on the refrigerator. He takes a couple of naps a day, and looks forward to our arrival home in the afternoon. He is able to concentrate for longer periods of time. If the body pain in his joints and muscles would subside, that

• • • •

would be a great blessing. His feet are still numb (side effect from the chemo), so no driving yet!

We are truly grateful for all the delicious meals that were delivered this month. We also received a number of gift cards to restaurants, so I think we are going to take a break in April and May from our dinner need on Mondays, Tuesdays, Wednesdays. When we know our surgery date for the colon surgery (Probably June), we will put up the calendar of meals again for those of you who would like to help out. I will let you know about yard work possibilities soon☺. Thanks for the generous offers!

May God continue to watch over each of you as you travel through this season of Lent. We are particularly aware of Christ's temptation and suffering this year... We were blind, but now we see.

Love,
Kathryn

PET scan
(A note from Kathryn)
Sunday, April 10, 2011, 9:45 PM

Dear Family and Friends,

We pray that you are all looking forward to spring and the new life that it brings. I think spring is finally here in Raleigh. We have had a week of April showers, and are awaiting the flowers! We are grateful for your continued prayers for our family and in particular

• • • •

Jerome's improved health. He has made significant gains over the past couple of weeks. Slow but sure. We are certain your support and prayers have played a major role in our recovery thus far. How blessed we have been to have you each with us.

We head into tomorrow's PET scan with the comfort of knowing that your prayers are surrounding us with God's love. Through that love, we will gain courage and strength to tackle whatever the results present. We meet with Dr. Yoffe on Wednesday.

Until then ~

May the Lord bless you and keep you!
May the Lord let His face shine upon you, and be gracious to you!
May the Lord look upon you kindly and give you peace!

Numbers 6:24-26

Great News!
(A note from Kathryn)
Wednesday, April 13, 2011, 5:00 PM

Praise the Lord!

The PET scan revealed NO LYMPHOMA!

The scan revealed hyper metabolic activity in the colon (cecum area). The scan last fall did not reveal this colon activity. At that time the cancer was microscopic. Dr. Yoffe explained that the area on the

• • • •

scan this week was more pronounced perhaps because (1) The cancer has grown, (2) The colon was irritated due to the chemo, and /or (3) Jerome's colitis is active. Dr. Yoffe was not concerned about the reasons, stating that the colon will be removed soon.

Jerome's surgery is tentatively planned for May 2nd at UNC. We will meet with Dr. Koruda on April 26th to determine the actual surgery and treatment schedule. When the colon is removed, doctors will then be able to determine the extent of the colon cancer and whether or not chemotherapy will be necessary between surgeries. We will keep you posted!

Thank you so much for the prayers, concern, and support. Each of you has made a huge difference in our lives. We are grateful. What a great day we have been given!

God Bless.
Kathryn

Chapter 11
Peace, Obedience, Grace

Joy of Life - Warm Wishes
(A note from Jerome)
Thursday, April 21, 2011, 10:30 PM

Dear Family & Friends,

You are such a blessing.

Our hearts are filled with a pure gratitude for you in our lives. I really wish I could sit down with each one of you so I could truly share the depth of our gratefulness. We are humbled by the many ways you have touched our family. The outpouring of your love through your prayers, cards, emails, meals, gifts to our family have filled us with such strength. You have been such an inspiration. You truly have reflected Christ's love for one another. Thank you from the center of our hearts and know the lasting smile you have given us through your love.

Tomorrow is Good Friday. Over the years, that day has become for me the most powerful renewal of my faith each year. It helps me feel connected to the cross and the gift of an amazing unconditional love that is like no other I have known. It is Christ's amazing love and story that inspires me in developing the relationships in my life. I have so many short comings, but this example keeps me asking for forgiveness where I fall short in my daily life. It renews me with the strength to awake and try again to give my best the next day. One of my favorite things to do on Good Friday comes at the end of the service. The large wooden crucified cross is laid before the altar for

• • • •

veneration, and the choir begins to sing songs that penetrate the soul. I stay seated in my pew listening to the music while taking time for deep reflection and witness. I witness the immense respect from people of all ages and backgrounds as they flow toward the cross to kiss, genuflect, or kneel with a prayer offering. They move humbly toward the cross offering their gratefulness and love for someone whose gifts have an unending timeless impact in their lives.

I saw this impact recently in the inspirational movie *The Pistol: The Birth of a Legend*. It is the true life movie story of Pistol Pete Maravich who was considered by many to have been one of the greatest basketball players to ever play the game. In this version of the movie, there were several extras features.

One extra feature was a recording of a powerful witness talk Pistol Pete gave in 1988 - three weeks before his death. The second was a witness talk by James Dobson, who held Pete in his arms after he collapsed on a basketball court. Seconds after Pistol told Dobson how great he felt, he collapsed and was gone within a minute.

During Pete's witness talk just weeks prior to his sudden death, he shared the amazing unparalleled story of his basketball fame and success. Then he shared the darkness behind the story of his life with his long battle with alcohol, drugs and other vices in his life. He searched the world over to find meaning in his life. When he found his faith he shared the strength and peace he had been looking for. One emotional pause came as he recalled the almost incomprehensible dichotomy of what took place with one of the world's greatest athletes. The second time he choked on his

• • • •

words was when he shared the conversation he had with his son when he returned home. Later that day Pete died.

I had Brock and Vince watch these witness talks with me. When the talks ended I shut off the TV and started to share with them the story of the day Kathryn and I were getting ready to give Vince his first haircut. Vince was shy of two at the time and was running all around the house giggling when the phone rang. I answered and it was my mother who said, "Oh Jerry, I think Dad's dead. He's so blue. Come quickly." I tossed the phone to Kathryn and told her to dial 911. I went running out of the house. I never saw my Dad alive again. He passed before I arrived.

As I looked into Brock and Vince's eyes after they had seen Dobson's witness talk and heard the story of my Dad's death, I saw an attentiveness I had never seen before. I then shared with them the thing I missed the most was that one last conversation with my Dad. It is why I gave the eulogy for my Dad at his funeral. It was my way of having that last conversation with him. I then shared with the boys my personal thoughts and wishes for them if my life was ever taken without warning. It was a particularly powerful moment for the three of us. We talked about the preciousness, the frailty, and the beauty of life.

Kathryn's inbox lit up like a Christmas tree with your email well wishes after she sent out the update a week ago with the PET scan results. Thank you for sharing in the goodness of that news. This morning I was the surprise story reader in Audrey's 1st Grade class. I also brought with me all the cards the kids had sent to me and sent to the hospital with Kathryn during

● ● ● ●

my Round 3. The cards had adorned my hospital door throughout my stay and brought big smiles to all who saw them. Even bigger smiles were seen this morning when I pulled out of my bag those same cards and went through each card with them thanking each student. I told them I would treasure their cards the rest of my life☺.

I have been going to water aerobics class daily at the YMCA on the advice of a friend. This is to help in the rebuilding of my strength. I am about 30-35% of my full strength. It was funny when I first started I went to AOA (Active Older Adults) basic class and there were twenty-two students. Twenty-one ladies with beautiful gray hair and, you guessed it, one guy with gray peach fuzz. It was especially nice and welcoming when in the middle of the class I was identified as the new student and was warmly greeted by my classmates. That was a *joy of life* moment☺.

Thank you again for everything you have done for our family. I head into surgery with a warm smile on my face. I have memories of you over the past several months and have warmth in my heart from your love, prayers and support. Wishing all of you a blessed and fun filled Easter and other traditions you celebrate with your family and friends. Thank you for everything and may the *joy of life* truly be yours.

Jerome

Jerome's Surgery

(A note from Kathryn),
Monday, May 2, 2011, 10:00 PM

Dear Family and Friends,

We thank you very much for your continued prayers. Your spirit of support was felt today by each of us! Here is a quick summary of today's events.

Jerome was scheduled for 7:30 AM surgery at UNC. We arrived at 6:00 AM and learned that our surgery would be delayed due to an emergency surgery in the OR. We waited and saw many medical representatives, and Jerome was able to go into surgery at 9:30 AM. He was done at 3:00 PM, but waited in recovery for about 4 hours while the nursing staff monitored his pain levels. The surgeon was pleased with the surgery. He did not see the cancer spreading outside of the colon (Yeah!! We are hopeful for this to be true!), but the pathology report will be complete on Friday or Monday. That report will determine whether or not chemo/radiation would be necessary (before the next surgery). Jerome was sleeping soundly when I left the hospital at 8:00 PM. Home by 9:00 PM. I was very grateful for Jerome's sister, Joan, for holding down the fort and doing homework with the kids afterschool. I will be back tomorrow.

Thank you for all you are doing for our family! I especially appreciated the well wishes, cards and fun surprises I received today to help make my birthday extra special! Having you all in our lives is reason for great celebration! You are gifts to us each day! Thank you for the time and energy you share!

• • • •

Please keep praying for:

(1) Reduced pain for Jerome;

(2) Patience for Jerome and me as we transition into use of the ileostomy bag;

(3) Increased strength for Jerome's body to heal well;

(4) Limited involvement of the cancer in the lining of the colon.

Thanks!

Love,
Kathryn and Jerome

Fantastic News
(A note from Kathryn),
Monday, May 9, 2011, 4:45 PM

Dear Subscribers☺,

The biopsy results revealed that Jerome's cancer had not penetrated through the colon wall! This is fantastic news, because this suggests that Jerome will not need more chemotherapy! Praise to God for this marvelous news. Yesterday the NG tube was removed and Jerome is feeling better today. The IV was taken out today, and he is easing back into normalcy (whatever that is!). We are grateful for all your continued support and care in calling and asking questions about Jerome's status at UNC over the past week. Not sure when the 'coming home' day is yet.

• • • •

Perhaps soon! I will let you know as soon as I know any more news.

We enjoyed a great Mother's Day. I hope you were able to celebrate the special day with a mom and/or a woman who has made a difference in your life! The kids let me sleep in, made me a fabulous frittata, accompanied me to visit Jerome, visited with Jerome's mom and sisters, went to pick strawberries, ate out at a great restaurant, and had many laughs! Our dear friend Jon is visiting from Seattle for a few days, and he has been a huge help on the homefront. He and Vince are presently planting vegetables and herbs out back. I am looking forward to cooking with them. A little bit of 'normal' for me!

God Bless,
Kathryn

Overcoming Anger's Shadows With Joy's Sunlight
(A note from Jerome)
Sunday, June 5, 2011, 11:15 PM

Dear Friends and Family,

It has been so great to be home these last several weeks healing and growing stronger. Your thoughts & prayers have definitely been felt and heard. Thank you!

This was the toughest hospitalization for me to go into. I had a lot of anger. Why? Well, this surgery was not something I ever wanted to have happen. It was

• • • •

more a defeat for me of sorts from a long fight. What many of you might not have known is that I had battled a disease in my colon called colitis for sixteen years with some very rough roads along the way resulting in several other hospitalizations from complications. My singular goal over the years was to keep the colitis from ever getting to a point of having colon surgery.

Back in 1995, I was given 0% odds of keeping my colon. Surgery appeared to be the only option as my colitis was in such bad shape. Those odds became a driving fuel for me. I drew hard upon my faith and sheer will to fight. Maybe my downfall was turning it around 16 years ago. I fought many battles since then along the way. But, finally, I reached the point last year, before any of the cancers were found, where I was told for the first time my colitis was inactive and my colon look great. "I made it!" I thought.

How cruel and ironic to hear that Stage 1 colon cancer had been found. Suddenly, there really were no more choices. Although the colitis was finally in check, it did not matter anymore. This new disease was a killer called cancer. Medical wisdom taught the only truly 100% successful way to treat colon cancer is to remove the entire colon. Unless I had the surgery, I was at risk. So, as the May 2nd surgery date approached there was a corresponding rise in my anger toward a surgery that I had worked so long, so hard, fought so many battles, endured daily so much to avoid. I wanted to leave this earth with all the parts God had created in me. This was not a 'Why me?' kind of anger. No, I have never felt that. This was a pure anger from not being able to do anything. I saw this colon surgery as a defeat. I had run the table on my options to keep all my parts.

• • • •

I could deal with the intense pain and discomfort following the colon surgery. What bothered me most was the anger I still felt inside. The true joy that was with me for so many months while I battled the lymphoma cancer was getting over shadowed by this anger. I desperately missed that joy. I was struggling to get it back. Toward the end of the first week in the hospital, I met someone who had defeated cancer through surgery, radiation, and chemo. When I shared with them what I was feeling, I received a surprise. After 10 years, this person was still angry over their cancer, their surgery and all they had to endure.

Suddenly, a switch was flipped. I found myself ministering to that anger. The more I talked, the more I let go. My words were strongly reverberating back to me. Trust. Faith. Joy. The more I gave and shared with this other person, the more I thought of them instead of myself. It was a gift! My anger was being reduced. Before the conversation was over, my anger was gone. As I reflected on it, there it was again... Mother Teresa's example to focus on others and their needs and the joy you receive will be endless. The Serenity Prayer is so rich in its wisdom upon reflection:

God grant me the serenity
to accept the things I cannot change;
courage to change the things I can
and wisdom to know the difference.

Where did this anger truly come from? I think it came from control. I was no longer in control of the colon fight. The cancer was. Unless I wanted to put myself and my family at risk by not having the surgery, there were no other options. The lesson I really learned

• • • •

was that I was focusing all these years on the wrong kind of control.

I was focused on control that was about me. A self-focus. A self-victory. No matter how I wanted to sugar coat it, the anger only came from me not being able to control something. I do not like anger. Nothing good I have found ever comes from it. I have never said anything that came from my mouth when I was angry that I liked or would not have said differently later when I was not angry. We have taught our children to count to ten if they are angry before speaking. If they are still angry, keep counting until the anger is gone... even if it take days.

My healing lesson here was the only valued control is the one where I control how I can reach out to others in need. This self-focus is very unfulfilling. This self-anger never generates anything of value. But, when we reach out and help others we truly live. God then graces us with a true and lasting joy that comes from living our lives in His son's image. You all have done that. By reaching out to our family with your many life giving thoughts, prayers and gifts you have touched our family's lives in so many healing ways. Thank you.

The second colon surgery right now is scheduled for June 22nd. I know enough to know this will be no cake walk. They will take down my ileostomy and the stoma, remove the last part of the colon which is my rectum, and then they will use part of my small intestine to form what is called a J Pouch which tries to take the place of my colon. I will learn a life style that will work for me. The surgeon said I will have pain and discomfort for about six months in my abdomen area as everything heals. Although I know there will be

• • • •
142

many challenges, I view it as a new beginning. I am ready for this 2nd surgery as it is the hurdle I must clear for the new life and health that I desire.

My focus will no longer be on this inner fight that has been a part of my life these past sixteen years. It will be on the ultimate gift of joy from learning how to live a life focused on others - Touching lives, practicing humility, and serving others through Christ's love.

Thank you for being God's light into our lives,
Jerome

Surgery Prayer Request
(A note from Kathryn),
Tuesday, June 21, 2011, 8:45 PM

Dear Friends and Family,

As we go into surgery tomorrow, we ask you to pray for patience (for me as I wait) and success (for Jerome to come through surgery with flying colors!). Jerome will check in at 11:00 AM. The surgery will begin at 1:00 PM at UNC Hospital. The surgery is about 5-6 hours. With that in mind, I may call and ask Kathy to update the website for me. I will stay with Jerome through recovery and his placement in his hospital room. It will be quite late when I get home.

Jerome was in good spirits today and this evening. I think he is ready. Knowing that you all are praying will carry Jerome through this step of the process. It is like

• • • •

our trip checklist we print out when we go to Wisconsin... We are packed and prepared for this journey. We have truly been blessed to have you all by our side as we have walked this road together. Many of you have sent responses to Jerome's Writings. Thank you. He and I have enjoyed hearing from you and sharing our family, faith, and life stories.

This Sunday is Jerome's 50th birthday. It is a great reason to celebrate and give thanks to the Lord! Maybe you have a thought or two to share with him as to what this journey has meant to you, and you'd like to share it with him on his birthday. Your friendship has been a treasured gift to Jerome (and to me!)

~ Thank you! Love, Kathryn

Surgery Goes Well
(A note from Kathryn),
Thursday, June 23, 2011, 10:15 AM

Praise to the Lord!

We felt your prayers. I really appreciated the gift of patience yesterday. The surgery was delayed for 2 1/2 hours, but Jerome and I passed the time playing cards. I let him win one round of Crazy Eights, but I lost track of how many hands we played☺. What a great distraction!!

Dr. Koruda came out at 7:45 PM and told me that he was very pleased with the results, and that everything went well. God is GREAT! I was able to go

• • • •

back and see Jerome at 11:00 PM in the recovery area. His color looked good. The nursing staff was managing his pain. They moved him up to #4716 shortly thereafter. I stayed with him until 12:15 AM. He was alert and working with the nursing staff to get as comfortable as possible for the night.

I am heading up to the hospital. Again, thank you for your continued prayers.

Love,
Kathryn

Jerome is Home
(A note from Kathryn),
Sunday, July 3, 2011, 9:15 AM

Dear Friends and Family,

Here is a quick update.

Jerome is home after the second surgery. The doctors were very pleased with the results. He has had a lot of pain, severe nausea, and has lost a lot of weight. He had some challenges when we arrived home, but the surgeon reassured us that it would take a few months for him to overcome them. We will take it one day at a time. He has severe pain in the tailbone, which affects most daily activities.

He is extremely grateful and really enjoyed the many letters you sent. He is humbled by the thoughts and feelings that were shared with him for his birthday.

• • • •

I surprised him by putting your letters in a binder for him to enjoy. If you would still like to send him a note, just send me an email. It is easy for me to add to his book!

Although this will be a long recovery, Jerome is extremely grateful for this new beginning. We could not have made this journey without your love, support, and prayers!

Have a blessed Fourth of July.

Love,
Kathryn

Joy of Life – Faith

(A note from Jerome)
Tuesday, August 16, 2011, 9:45 PM

Dear Family & Friends,

Thank you.

Those words barely roll off my tongue when I already feel a strong internal desire to find a better way to express our gratitude. I can never seem to find all the words to say '*Thank you'* with all the ways that it is felt in our hearts. The feelings are there because of the many ways you have and continue to touch our family's lives with your most genuine love.

This was a rough round. The cumulative effect of all the chemotherapies and surgeries took a real physical and mental toll. This time in the hospital I had almost reached my mental end after not eating for seven straight days after surgery because of severe nausea that hounded me day and night. Physically I weighed in at 145 pounds. When I came home, severe tailbone and sciatic pain set in lasting for the first few weeks.

Last week after feeling like my recovery was continuing to be such a struggle to regain my strength and some form of energy, my oncologist shared with me that my feelings were validated when the results from my blood tests showed anemic blood which he encouraged will heal over time. Yet, today all of those challenges feel so distant. They seem minimal and so trivial. Yesterday, I was powerfully reminded of the true essence in life. How to live with the kind of love demonstrated by a little girl I was honored to know.

• • • •

Love. Real love. You know when it is present. It touches you in just the right way. Just when you need it most. It comes with purity from one another in our words and actions bringing a joy and healing to hearts with a gentle kindness. Throughout this journey I have witnessed so much love in so many incredible forms, but none more evident than yesterday when love's most beautiful form was on display.

If you were there in that full church at St. Francis you felt, really felt, love in its purest form. God's design in our lives. All of it explainable? No. Its origin? A six year old little girl name Faith whose *Joy of Life* was written all over her face. Not only in her infectious smile, but so much more in her eyes that penetrated right from her heart to yours.

God had given this little girl a special heart. Her heart pulsed a pure love directly from God. Not in a perfect physical form but in something much greater touching deeply into one's soul. Her physical heart, that ultimately could not be healed and stopped beating a few days ago on August 10th, had been replaced with a heart that really taught those around her to yearn to live each day with her kind of love. A love that makes eyes mist with powerful emotions. It stops your breath deep within your chest with its forceful pause of how special life is. It shows most importantly a child's kind of innocence and passionate love for the people and moments we are blessed with each day.

This little girl named Faith taught me the kind of love that God intends each of us to live by each day. Faith's love is an inspiration to me. All I wanted to do yesterday as I hugged her mom and dad was trade places with Faith so they could have more time with

• • • •

her. Their love for her was beyond measure. Her mother is an inspiration. Several months ago she stood with Kathryn and me in our kitchen with a warm meal. She shared the struggles that Faith was experiencing, yet there she was showing us love with her encouraging presence in our home.

Faith's whole family was an inspiration validated by a full church of loving family and friends. Yesterday, Faith's father and oldest sister stood up in front of the church at Faith's funeral and shared with us words of welcome and remembrance. Their strength and trust in God's design were real inspiration. Their pain - deep. Their voice - trusting. Their love for a daughter, a sister, a friend - the kind to emulate.

This whole journey has been an inspiration for life as God intends. My sufferings have only sharpened my deep awareness of my shortcomings and how much more there is in living this gift of life in the right way. God's strong words in my head and his firm hand on my reluctant back to share these thoughts with an openness and honesty that puts it all out have not been easy. However, the way you have responded helped me understand the power of his design if we let it flow through us without trying to control it. It has also been incredible to see what our family has experienced from your collective souls. It has been felt deeply in our hearts and has been so very inspirational and humbling. You have honored our family with your presence in this journey. You have shown us the kind of goodness of a pure love that truly exists in all of us. I have let God's design sometimes get lost in life's distractions or had it fall down on my focus list. It is not easy to live as God intends us to live. It is easy to fall back into old habits. To let life challenges and pressures take control of you in undesired directions

• • • •

with feelings, words and actions that do not reflect this right kind of love. But, each night my knees hit the ground praying for renewed strength, and I hope that tomorrow I can do a little better to live out His presence in me, in my words, and in my actions.

All our best to you and your families. I will try to check in again with you sometime around Christmas. Right now I am inspired to continue to try to get fully healed so I can honor Faith's life by how I live mine. For each day we are given an opportunity for how we will be remembered... the opportunity each day brings by just really living that day for the moments it brings with the kind of love for one another taught to me by a little girl named Faith who put her heart in mine.

Love you,
Jerome

Joy of Life - All Clear... God's Way

(A note from Jerome)
Sunday, January 29, 2012, 9:30 PM

Dear Family & Friends,

"All clear..."

One thing this experience has taught me is to allow for the unexpected... When it comes... Well, it is still sometimes hard to hear.

A couple weeks ago I received the results of my most recent CAT Scans. Initially, I felt some strong emotions that really surprised me. The news brought more unknowns as the result of new findings. The results found what they termed a hypo dense region on my liver which is "concerning for metastatic disease or possible primary hepatic neoplasm." It is on the left lobe of my liver. They cannot do a needle or surgical biopsy to do further analysis and diagnosis because the region is too vascular. There would be a high risk of hemorrhage with those procedures. The doctors are not sure if the hypo dense region is something caused by trauma from my surgeries or if it is metastatic cancer or if it is primary liver cancer. They have to give it more time to see if or how it changes. I will be scheduled for a full body PET scan toward the end of March. They will also do a bone density scan.

This news blindsided me. I had prepared myself to hear many things in the report but this was not one of them. Just when we thought we might be getting the 'all clear' signal, we needed to reach deeper for more patience.

● ● ● ●

A blessed virtue that I continue to realize eludes me at times during this experience. I have it, even strongly, at times... and then life seems to twists itself in unexpected turns and once more the chase is on to recapture it. Let go and let God... I continue my journey on how to learn to do this well from another dear friend who gave me a precious treasure in a book entitled *The Gift of Faith* by Father Tadeusz Dajczer. I can only read a little bit each day as there is so much to absorb and reflect upon. It is filled with encouragements and clarity of letting go, completely trusting, totally surrendering... These are the areas that I have found require daily focus in one's faith to grow to a level God allows us to go to for a sanctuary of complete peace.

Life's twists can bring powerful struggles to keep that peace. One's focus has to be unrelenting against the forces that try to rip that peace away from you. Although these new scan findings with their possibilities bring again that huge variance, from being something of mild concern that will heal over time (surgical trauma) to something that can easily take one's life with these two types of possible cancers. It is really these unknowns that I have to let go of as I am not in control of that. If I really believe God's plan is the best for me, then I need to embrace whatever He puts in my life's path as His methods of forging and pounding me into His perfect design.

We shared the news with Brock, some of it with Vince, but we did not have the heart or thought it wise to share with Gretchen & Audrey. We do not have enough information at this point to really know what we are dealing with. The medical experts say it is most likely surgical, but I have been on the opposite side of that 'most likely' too many times through this experience. You cannot let yourself go one way or

• • • •

another. You just have to be patient until more is known. More importantly, you have to truly trust and feel like a child in God's arms. It is such a motivating image to me of how a child really lives the moments of each day with such great trust. I pray for this child-like level of faith every time I say the rosary.

Yes, as I admitted, at first the news was very rough to hear. I have since started to recover and am doing much better as my faith adjusts, grows and strengthens to absorb another twist in life that I did not see coming. Recently I unfortunately have developed some strong bursitis in my left shoulder from trying to push my cancer recovery workouts too hard. I have been taking it easy these past couple of weeks to try to let that heal. It has been another reminder of how precious our health is. I am smiling while I continue this twisting path of life. I feel God's love and yours. Overall, it has not been the smooth slope I had hoped for. Rather, a much different and much more challenging plan for me that builds my character the best way... God's way.

Our family continues to feel the incredible grace and strength from all of your prayers. Thank you. May God's graces bless you and your families with true lasting joy.

Jerome

The Lenten Journey Continues

(A note from Kathryn),
Wednesday, March 14, 2012, 9:15 PM

Dear Friends and Family,

We pray all is well with each of you. Foremost, we continue to be grateful for all the prayers and continued support from each of you for the improvement of Jerome's health. As many of you know, tomorrow was to be Jerome's PET scan; we were waiting for an 'all clear' sign of great health! There has been a delay.

Last Thursday, I took Jerome to the ER at 2:00AM in the morning with severe dehydration, vomiting, and cramping. It was determined that he had a bowel obstruction. After 18 hours in the ER, he stayed overnight at Rex and was then transported to UNC for further evaluation. He has been there since last Friday. This past week has brought much pain and many questions resulting in several procedures, scans, and tests. I've been trying to keep the kids' schedules and routine as normal as possible. They are doing well.

Tomorrow Jerome will have an ERCP procedure to look at his upper GI tract and liver. Join us in prayer that the doctors find the reasons for Jerome's discomfort and offer us some possible solutions to aid in his healing.

God is the Divine Healer. We are confident in his plan. I am grateful for the reminder of that fact. Thanks, Pat.

Love to you, Kathryn

••••

Jerome is Home - An Easter Blessing
(A note from Kathryn),
Saturday, March 31, 2012, 4:30 PM

After three weeks in the hospital, Jerome is home! He is resting in his own bed. Unfortunately the ERCP procedure led to Jerome having pancreatitis. As you may know, pancreatitis is extremely painful. He has a constant stabbing pain in his back and abdomen. He is trying to manage the pain; however, it is really difficult. He gets little rest and very little relief. He has lost about twenty pounds, and has had little to no appetite to regain some of those pounds. I have offered to donate, but he has not taken me up on that offer! He has started eating Frosted Flakes, so things might be looking up soon☺.

The liver still holds many questions. Further testing is needed to develop a better understanding of the hyper dense mass that was originally seen on Jerome's liver in December. We hope to get a better direction of a treatment plan when we visit the doctor next week. Jerome is resting and trying to get stronger. Thank you all so much for your continued prayers. We are so blessed to have each of you in our faith circle! Prayers for pain relief would be welcomed. We also would like to pray that the doctors could find a winning game plan for Jerome to return to full health!

Speaking of game plan... Jerome had a huge smile on his face today when Vince called his dad to report that he shot 24/25 free throws to win the Knights of Columbus State Free Throw Championship in Burlington, NC! Nothing brings it home for Jerome like a basketball success story!

●●●●

As we enter Holy Week, we remember the Passion of our Lord and the incredible joy that Easter brings. Jesus gives us the Hope for a brighter tomorrow. We are forever grateful!

Love,
Kathryn

Chapter 12
Surrender, Trust, Lasting Joy

Joy of Life - The Pause
(A note from Jerome)
Sunday, July 15, 2012, 10:30 PM

Dear Family and Friends,

"The great thing is..." That was the discussion prompt in one of my cancer survivor group discussions. As the leader put that prompt to the group to spur the start of our discussion several people started right away sharing their responses... "... to be cancer free...", "... all the support I received from family and friends..." As I listened to their thoughts, I reflected hard for my answer. What was 'the great thing' I felt inside from my experiences? I did not know if I was cancer free so that could not be it. Family and friends, yes, of course, but why so much more now? My faith, yes, that too, but what had caused it to deepen? Toward the end of the discussion I simply said with a smile, "The pause."

The great thing is... The Pause. Simple, but its power has turned my world upside down. As I reflected for that true feeling inside of me that was my answer. What kept coming into my mind was how this tremendous pause forced itself into my life without permission. It has changed my life completely. I will never be the same. I will never think of any day as ordinary. Every person I encounter each day and every moment is a gift. I must be wise with how I treat people and each opportunity. In the midst of my suffering I have learned to smile and laugh. This gift of powerful pauses comes with lessons that never seem to cease. I let them flow into and through me. I finally let go of control to hear God's voice in my life. He had and has a lot to say.

My days now are so different. There is so much I cannot control. I am faced daily with such a different set of realities that have led me to look at each moment of each day with this new kind of pause. This pause stopped the life I was living and started a new life where faith is my constant companion. The new life is filled with trust and surrendering. The new life has taught new levels of humility and patience I did not know even existed.

The experiences of these past years have taught me what true suffering really is with its gripping, incapacitating pain at times. There are days when this incapacitating suffering comes, and it comes again, and again... 33 times was the most in one day of this torturing incapacitating challenge.

My mind has been pushed toward the edge of the cliff where I just wanted to jump off to stop the pain. When this happens, I reach and grasp for my faith with a shaking hand. With a clenched fist I swallow hard for the continued fight. I do not let myself go near the edge because I feel the strength returning to my body. It is an answer to prayer to continue the fight.

I have learned that only through faith will you find the mental strength you require to combat all of this which seems so unbelievably limitless at times in its

● ● ● ●
158

cruelty. It is no match for the indescribable comfort that awaits once you discover that the source of love and strength from God is truly eternal.

In March, after a month long stay at UNC Hospital, I found out that I have an incurable liver disease. There is no way to treat it, to slow it, or to reverse it. It is a progressive disease whose power has the capability of shutting down my liver someday. The only option would be a transplant if I were a candidate. I am not. Because of my oncology and medical history, a transplant is not in the cards for me. The disease is called Primary Sclerosing Cholangitis (PSC). It is considered a chronic disease. It inflames and scars the bile ducts of the liver. The inflammation and scarring impedes the flow of bile to the digestive system.

PSC is progressive. It ultimately can lead to liver cirrhosis, liver failure, and/or liver cancer. Life expectancy on average of people with this disease is 7 to 12 years, but can vary greatly. My oncologist has a patient that has had it over 20 years. They cannot tell me what percent of my ducts are scared or when it started. They did tell me that both my small and large bile ducts are affected, which poses a higher risk for more serious symptoms. Unfortunately, an additional complication of PSC is that it has the potential to turn into bile duct cancer. This is a type of cancer I did not even know existed. It is a quick killer.

The medical knowledge on the percentage of times bile duct cancer arises in PSC patients varies widely depending on the source. Most sources put it at 7-12%, but Mayo Clinic says, "Up to 30 percent of people diagnosed with primary sclerosing cholangitis will eventually develop cancer in their bile ducts." Ultimately, the percentages do not matter. There are

• • • •

so many variables, and my set of health complications have taken me off the statistical grid of meaningful comparisons. If bile duct cancer would arise it can be treated with chemo and radiation, but this will only slow the disease. Yes, you can do surgery to cut out the cancer depending upon how much of the liver is affected, but it is a very complex surgery with many high risk factors. Unfortunately, my PSC would remain. So, if this complication would arise in the future surgery is not an attractive option when you weigh the immediate loss of quality of life that comes with chemo and radiation against just living as long as you can without it. As crazy and humorous as it sounds, none of the above is my current concern or challenge. Those are just possible future challenges.

The thing that put me in the hospital in March and again on Father's Day is something called Pelvic Floor Dyssynergia. This means the muscles and nerves that help me go to the bathroom are not communicating and working properly creating numerous challenges. The dyssynergia could be from the chemo, the surgeries to remove my colon, or a combination of both. The doctors are not really sure. The challenge it presents is enormous. I struggle with going to the bathroom and then if things get worse and stop working, I can quickly find myself uncontrollably vomiting, getting dehydrated by the minute, and knowing the only course of treatment is going to be a trip to the ER.

Why did things stop working in March? Looking back, it probably was not something that suddenly occurred but rather was a slow buildup from the combination of many factors. Biofeedback is a current option for hope. I am going through a series of biofeedback sessions to try to retrain the muscles and

●●●●

nerves to work in synergy again. Treatment can take up to 6 months and has about a 70% success rate. With some of those muscles being voluntary and some involuntary, it is a tricky, slow process that is testing my patience. I am really praying at some point I will turn the positive corner to restore some kind of normal function. We are also trying diets of different types and supplements. The host of complicating health factors that have arisen from this each day challenges me to re-energize, smile and grit my teeth. I have no idea what it will bring.

Pause.

I thought my purpose was to be here in our children's lives at the graduations, the special events, the milestones. I realize that I may not be there the day Brock graduates from Notre Dame and is commissioned as an officer in the Navy. I may not be there to talk through career choices with Vince. I may not see Gretchen graduate high school, go to college, or turn that magical age of 21. I may not be there to walk Audrey down the aisle at her wedding. I realize that if I am not there it all is going to be okay. It is going to be okay because I had the honor of being the Eucharistic Minister at their First Holy Communions. What a special moment to give your child the Body of Christ. I now know they already have faith in God. It is the greatest gift Kathryn and I could ever impart upon them. Faith.

This faith will guide, watch over, and inspire. They can turn to faith at any time in the future for the right advice in their lives. Our children do not have to have my presence to fully live or to help achieve moments in their lives. They have learned a lesson of a lifetime from what we have learned and experienced as a

• • • •

family. It is only through faith that you get to savor and enjoy all that life has to offer. You simply need faith to fully live. The Pause taught us all powerful lessons inspired by God.

I have had some people tell me that I am an inspiration to them or one of the strongest people they know. I have met many other people through this experience where I pale in comparison. Let me share the story of one with you.

Moments.

Do you know what you were doing or what happened on March 28, 2004? I suspect like me you do not, but my friend Bruce can recall that day in vivid detail. His phone rang, and it was someone from a hospital in Orlando, Florida. He needed to get on a plane immediately. His daughter Lauren was in the emergency room in extremely critical condition. Lauren was born on August 24, 1981, in Raleigh. She graduated from Millbrook High School in 2000. She was due to graduate from college on May 10, 2004. She had recently completed an internship in New York City, where she planned to start her career. Lauren was a beautiful young woman who was full of energy, life, and love for all those around her. She exuded her love of God by how she lived. At such a young age she had already touched many lives.

When Bruce arrived in Orlando and was in a cab rushing to the hospital his phone rang again. He did not make it in time to hold her hand, to give her that kiss, to tell her that he was there. The doctor said he was so sorry, but Lauren had passed away from massive injuries sustained in a car crash.

● ● ● ●

Lauren was headed down to a cruise ship for a fun Spring Break when suddenly debris from a retreaded tire caused the fatal crash. On May 10, 2004, at the college graduation ceremony at the University of Alabama, the presider called out the names of the graduates. At one point he announced, "Lauren Allyn Braddy" Only her gown of remembrance was there that day along with the tears in all of her friend's and family's eyes.

Enjoy the moments each day. Savor every one. No day is an ordinary day.

Another phone call. This time weeks before the crash. Bruce's 'one in a million' daughter was calling him to make a request. Would he be her date for a dance? There were a long line of men that would love to have asked her to the dance, but she was calling to ask her dad to be her date. Bruce said, "Yes," with a broad smile. I held Lauren's framed picture in my hands as Bruce was sharing this story. He had a beautiful mist in his eyes as he shared how he flew down to the University of Alabama for that weekend of smiles, twirls, food and fun. He did not have a clue it would be his last dance with his daughter. Moments. Enjoy them each day. Savor every one. No day is an ordinary day.

What is God asking us to do? When I open my heart and listen, it is so simple. Love, care and enjoy one another. Each day we are presented with opportunities to serve, to help somebody, to make a difference in a life, to bring a smile or to laugh with someone.

We can get lost from even seeing these moments by living what sometimes can be termed as a *me first* life. I have been guilty many times of this in my life. God calls each of us to serve and bring out the best in one another. For me it starts by having outward focus. To remind myself of this focus, I ask God to increase my knowledge of Him and His plan for my life. I take a drop of holy water by my bed that someone had given to me from Lourdes. I touch my eyes and pray to really see the opportunities that await me that day. I touch my nose and ask for help to understand right from wrong. I touch my ears and ask to be able to listen with understanding of what others are saying to me and feel the meaning in their words. I touch my mouth and ask that the words that I choose will bring out the best in others. I smile while reminding myself of God's wisdom as he designed us with two eyes, two ears and only one mouth. Please help me to observe and listen much more than I speak. Finally, I touch my heart and I ask God to help me love others as I feel His love for me.

From all of my experiences, I can honestly say that mentally I feel like an Olympian. Not in the champion or greatness sense, and certainly, certainly not in the physical sense – LOL. No, it is the struggle and endurance that an Olympian must bring to train and discover the personal best that is within. For me, my suffering has been my personal trainer. It has stretched me so far beyond where I ever was and has challenged every part of my soul to turn over control and trust to God as my sole source of strength.

I never knew until recently that one of the people whom I hold the deepest respect for suffered greatly from disease in his life. Who was this person? Not just a person, but a Saint. Saint Francis. Again, my suffering pales in comparison to his, but I was encouraged by how he used his suffering to deepen his

● ● ● ●

faith to a level I can only aspire. Does that mean we have to suffer to become a Saint or to become holy? No, not even close. It does mean we need to understand the teachings and the lessons from the sufferings of Christ. He was the ultimate role model. Each of us has Christ within us. He can come out of us through the actions and words we choose to do and say each day. That is how we can really love and care for one another at a whole new level. Each day we can renew our attitude of an outward focus to bring out the best within each other.

I started reading recently from a book that talks about how challenges in our life are like a giant enormous rock in our path. Our first thought is to go around, over, or under it to get by. But, it is so big that none of these options work. What are we left to do with this enormous rock in our path? As a dear friend of mine who lost her battle with cancer said, "Embrace it!" The rock is God. It is only through Him that we can survive - not only in this lifetime but in the ultimate opportunity that awaits.

My Bible knowledge is just above ignorance. So, I was excited to learn an inspiring story of suffering in the Bible that I never knew. This book is considered appropriately one of the books of wisdom – Job. No one really knows who Job was, but he came along long before Christ. He was a very rich man blessed with children, and had his health. Without warning it was all taken away – his wealth, his children, and he was left to suffer with an incredibly painful disease. He had every reason to be bitter and to turn away from God.

My friend Bruce also had a crossroads decision after Lauren tragically died. Which path would he take? Like Job, he managed to keep his faith. Does it

• • • •

mean we do not ever question God? Pain from suffering or pain from loss runs so deep it forces that question at some point. What do we choose when pain runs so deep that you're just left numb from it all. How could and did Job and Bruce not only stay men of faith, but then turn and actually evangelize faith from their pain? I am not sure, but that is what faith is. It takes on its greatest form when we have to turn and surrender completely. We must 'embrace' the rock. We must be patient beyond reason and hope without question marks to reach that level of trust so that we can give ourselves to the rock in our path. That is what we need to do so that one day we will not go around, over, or under the rock, but we will live through it and only it. Yes. It is very hard to do.

Start today with a wife or a husband, a sister or a brother, a daughter or a son, a friend or a stranger. Let them know how much you care, how much you love them, how very sorry you are for a wrong you made. Make someone laugh. Remember Mother Teresa's words, "Unless a life is lived for others, it is not worthwhile." John Wooden used that quote throughout his life. People call him the greatest sports coach that ever lived. Well, let us learn from him and other people of greatness. What is common between them? They were humble. They focused and served others first. They were deeply faith-filled. There were great challenges in their lives. They trusted God.

Each day we are given opportunities to coach by using our example as the teaching tool. What style will we choose? How can we bring out the best in those around us each day? Listen for that voice inside that is trying to get out. It is waiting for each of us to give it control and to trust it with our lives. Bruce's story tells us that we never know what a day may bring. The

• • • •

only thing we really control is to 'let go' and allow ourselves to live as God intends. For me now, it is not again, again, and again. Rather, it is pause, pause, and pause. I need to remember who is in control, and who I have given control to. No matter what this life brings.

Thank you for being such a gift in our lives. You make me smile.

I recently shared with Vince that I was going to be sending out an update to everyone. I wanted him to hear the details of my health situation first from me. As we were sitting outside on the porch talking, a mist filled his eyes as he started to understand the situation. One of the special things we talked about were all of the wonderful people in our lives. We talked about our family being surrounded by people who loved and cared for us. When good or bad things happen, we will not be alone. We have each other. We have God.

It is very humbling when someone comes up to me and says, "Just want you to know I am still praying for you..." I am touched when I receive a card in the mail or an email note that says, "Hey just wanted you to know I did this and wanted to say thanks for..." I am grateful for the unexpected gift that lands in our lap when we need it most. Kathryn and I look at each other with a 'God's hand' look. When the phone rings with a call from a friend who wanted to share a laugh, we join in the laughter.

You have touched our family in so many unexpected ways. You have been living angels who have strengthened our children with your examples of love and kindnesses. You have brought out our best.

Thank you and God Bless you!! ~Jerome

• • • •

Prayer Request

(A note from Kathryn),
Wednesday, August 15, 2012, 10:15 PM

Dear Family and Friends,

The summer is coming to an end. Brock enjoyed his four week Navy CORTRAMID experience/training in San Diego. The kids and I had fabulous times at Camp Monterey in Tennessee (Thank you Mary Grace!) and in Seattle (Danke, Jon und Hartmut). We all loved the time in Raleigh with many of the Friedman family during our reunion in July. Those times with family and friends have given us a renewed strength to face the news of today.

As many of you are aware, Jerome has had many physical challenges since March. This past week we have been to the Emergency Room twice. Presently at Rex Hospital, Jerome has had pain meds and is somewhat comfortable as he prepares for tomorrow.

I ask for your prayers especially for the coming days. Tomorrow Jerome has a GI procedure to relieve some discomfort and a biopsy for a mass on his abdomen that has increased in size (20-30%) since May. We also pray for some guidance in our next steps of the treatment plan. As Jerome continues to experience intestinal tract problems, we are especially grateful to Jacques (our brother-in-law) for his knowledge and efforts in working with our doctors to explore the best options for Jerome. When we get past the biopsy results, we will let you all know what our next step may be and how best to pray. For your continued faith, friendship, and hope ~ Thank you.

•••

I am driving Brock up to Notre Dame Saturday and returning Sunday. So please add 'safe travels' to the prayer list. Go Irish!

Love,
Kathryn

Quick Update on Jerome
(A note from Kathryn),
Thursday, August 30, 2012, 9:15 PM

I am writing a brief note to update you on the latest news regarding Jerome's health. I say brief, because I need some rest, yet I know many have asked what to pray for. I so thank you for your notes, prayers, impromptu dinners. They all have made a difference! The kids are grateful especially for the food☺. So yes, I will be asking Kathy to post a sign-up for a few meals per week while Jerome undergoes chemotherapy. You have asked, and I am saying, "Yes!" (with reservation), but great thanksgiving. The sign-ups may go up next week.

The past two weeks have brought much uncertainty as test results were compared, discussed, and questioned. The problems Jerome has had with his J pouch this summer have been stabilized and put on the back burner for the time being. The stomach mass reveals itself as what appears to be a third cancer attacking Jerome's body, but the primary origin of the cancer is not known. The cancer is thought to be biliary duct cancer. Jerome's case has been quite complex due to his other cancers and surgeries. We are truly

• • • •
169

grateful to the doctors, nurses, and the Rex community for providing such excellent care. Tomorrow Jerome will transfer back to the opposite 5th floor wing, have a port-a-cath implanted and start chemotherapy. Assuming Jerome can tolerate the chemo, the treatment plan will be re-evaluated in 6 weeks. We are hopeful that he will be able to come home in between treatments.

Please continue to pray for strength for all of us. We ask that God grants wisdom and guidance to the physicians so that they can best treat Jerome. We pray that God's Will be done, and that we will trust and be grateful for the blessings He gives us each day. That is a tall order, I know. Jerome and I celebrated our 25th wedding anniversary yesterday. We were able to spend some of the evening sharing our favorite memories of our 30 years together. We have been so blessed with fantastic people and great joy in our lives. Thank you for being by our side.

Have a safe weekend.

Love,
Kathryn

Prayer to God
(A note from Jerome)
September 23, 2012

Recently I had one of the worst and most painful days that I have had in a long time. Severe lasting pain followed by abdominal cramping. It was not a quick cramp. It lasted from about 9 o'clock the previous night through the next day. I did not go into the emergency room because it was the day of Vince's homecoming dance. The kids were coming over to the house to take pictures. I wanted to be here. I tried to deal with the pain the best I could. I took some extra pain medication. Eventually, through all the efforts, the pain started to ease up a little bit. When I went to bed, I still was in so much pain Kathryn had to dress me. I could not even kneel down and say my prayers. I got up a couple of times in the middle of the night. When I got up the fourth time, I was in a position where I could slide off and let my knees hit the floor and say my prayer.

Dear God,

Thank You for the gifts of yesterday - The gift to connect with your suffering on the cross and better understand the pain and suffering that you endured for me and the rest of mankind. I understand how obedient you were to your Father's request to pay for all the sins of mankind through that suffering. I cannot even imagine what it must have felt like to go through that kind of pain. That kind of suffering. And not for something that you did, but for something that someone else did. That is having a true work focus. You were not thinking of yourself, but you were thinking of me, my brother, my sister, my friends. Your

● ● ● ●

sacrifice, your suffering, the pain that you endured, all was for others. You did it in the humblest of ways. You did it without raising a word or a fist. You did it with love in your heart - an unconditional, endless, deep, abiding love in your heart. Yes God, thank you for the gift of yesterday with its pain and suffering to help me understand more the gift of your son, Christ, for me. And what he endured for the forgiveness of my sins. As I approach this new day, help me with renewed strength to greet this day and all it may bring. I love you God with all my heart. Thank you for the gift of one more day.

Joy of Life - Unimaginable
(A note from Jerome)
Friday, October 5, 2012, 1:30 AM

Dear Family & Friends,

One twenty-nine. A number that I never thought I would see again in my life. 129. The number that stared back at me when I stepped on the scale. 129 pounds.

Hospice came and met with us two weeks ago. You could have asked me to name a million things I would do in 2012. Meeting with Hospice in our home would never have entered my mind. That was unimaginable. So was the emergency room visit in August with major problems and extraordinary pain throughout my abdomen. Cancer. When they said it, it was heard with disbelief. I had just had my scans done not that long ago. The problem was a tumor that had grown in size by 20-30% and was now being referred to as possibly cancerous.

It is unimaginable that one would hope for colon cancer. Yet that is what Kathryn and I found ourselves doing days later as the doctors worked through what this tumor was. Hoping for colon cancer? You have got to be kidding me. Why would you hope for that? My oncologist delivered to Kathryn and I (with tears in his eyes and a broken heart) that the pathology news came back as a Stage 4 cancerous tumor in my abdomen of unknown primary origin. Colon cancer gave us the most hope.

I asked my oncologist in his 30 years of experience how many patients he had had with my three cancers (colon, lymphoma, and bile duct cancer). He paused

• • • •

looking up thinking and then replied with a shaking head, "One... You." I later asked one of my surgeons how many patients he ever knew who had three distinct types of cancers. "A handful," he said with a voice of compassion and disbelief at our medical challenges.

'Beyond surreal' is the way that Kathryn describes our experiences since the middle of August. No matter what you do in life, nothing prepares you for this kind of experience. But only one thing gets you through it, your faith. My mother said to me, "I'm praying for a miracle." I responded to my mother, "Mom, I think we are witnessing a miracle."

I said once before in an earlier writing, this is not about me, this is about all of us. This has been a collective journey for all of us involved. I could tell you a thousand stories of how I have felt God's presence and hand throughout all of this. It comes from those little ways that could only have been orchestrated by God's amazing design for our lives. How do I recognize His presence? It comes through you, your words, your actions at just the right moment.

Now this unpredictable journey all makes sense. I realize that the miracle that has been unfolding all along is all of you. When I reflect and pray about this journey, it is clear to me that God has been performing a living miracle through all of us since the beginning of my illness. God has been weaving our lives together as only He can. How else can one explain the beautiful thoughts that I distinctly heard with their powerful meaning and impact to life? How else can one be so blessed with countless cards, letters, emails, and prayers? I wish you could read all of the responses as they stand as living proof of this miracle that is

• • • •

transforming relationships in our lives. You have shared how this journey has touched you, inspired you, made you more appreciative, more patient, more loving, more giving, more grateful, more aware. Changes like these only come from one true source. When we allow God to enter our hearts and minds, He starts to chisel us into His image when we give Him the hammer.

How much, how incredibly much, Kathryn and I have longed and wish we could respond personally to each and every one of you. We have felt your presence next to us as we have taken each step in this unpredictable, unrelenting and now unimaginable journey. Your love has been so genuine, so abundant, so unending that words cannot possibly capture the incredible impact each of you has made. Each night as my legs slide down off the bed and my knees hit the floor, I find myself in deep prayer joyously expressing to God an unending gratitude for the gift of you in our family's lives.

We have learned together to follow Mother Teresa's inspirational example of not asking what is needed in one another's lives, but seeing a need and just responding to it with the unique gifts that God has blessed us with. How incredible our world would be if each day we could all remind ourselves to live in the footsteps of this beautiful woman. A Saint whose humble existence not only touched those she reached out to when she saw a need, but also changed hearts with her living example. Her example spread throughout the world with simplicity and magnificence of how just one life, with random acts of kindness, intertwined with others, can touch millions worldwide.

Mother Teresa left the comforts, the security, the walls and confines of the Church to reach out and to go

• • • •

out into the community. She saw the need and longed to fulfill those needs. I had a much similar experience when this cancer journey began. I had to leave the safety and security of my privacy to share not only my health news, but my life, my vulnerabilities, my shortcomings, my faith, and the changes within myself. As I shared more, as I went deeper into the Writings, your responses came back more personal and profound. It has left me forever changed in the best of ways. The most incredible part of Mother Teresa's story was that she was an ordinary woman who took a risk on an idea without having all the answers. She lived out her mission in an extraordinary way. Each of us has the opportunity to live as Mother Teresa did. Not in replication of its exactness but by the attitude with how we look upon and treat one another. That is the power of her lesson.

I believe that is what changed my mentor John Wooden. He listed Mother Teresa as one of the greatest mentors in his life. He let her example forever change him in how he lived his life. Reading about both of their lives helped me to appreciate the changes in my life that needed to be made. We always retain our uniqueness as individuals. God put each of us together differently. How we treat, how we talk, and how we act with each other allows us to absorb qualities from each other and chisel each other into Christ's image.

I do not pray for a miracle. If I prayed that way, and received a different outcome, then my prayer request might be construed as a disappointment. Perhaps God did not deliver on my prayer. In reality, it may be that God has not delivered results according to my plan. That perspective on prayer I refer to as a 'gray faith'. It is a faith that only trusts to a certain level, or a faith that only surrenders so far and then

● ● ● ●

tries to take back control. I do not want a gray faith. I want a black and white faith that fully gives everything I have to God. So, rather than praying for a specific miracle, I pray for strength. I pray for understanding. I pray to draw closer to God and to bring out the Christ within. I pray to learn how to fully surrender and to fully trust.

An outcome from this past hospitalization was a constant encouraging voice from all of you to write and record these *Joy of Life* thoughts. Having made the decision now to write the story gives me such an internal purpose. One part of the purpose is to respond to you by accepting your challenge to write the *Joy of Life.* The other reason is to give a future voice to my children that they can come back to as they grow older. The book will continue to speak to them about the most important life lessons I have come to know.

One of the best books I have ever read is *Illusions*. As I have continued to read it over the years, I have found that it speaks to me differently as I add my own life experiences and wisdom. Each time I read it, I better understand the book, its messages, and teachings for my life. It is funny. The words in the book never change, yet their meaning becomes much clearer to me. I guess that is how we acquire true wisdom as we age. Things that we could not fully appreciate or understand when we were young all of a sudden seem to be such wise advice when we are older.

You are bringing out the best in me by what you have done during this unimaginable journey. It has taken us all on this rollercoaster called *LIFE* with its highs and lows, twists and turns, fears and joy. When we boarded together in that first writing I sent out to you, I clearly had no idea where I was going. Now I am

●●●●

seeing the greatest light I have ever seen with colors and beauty I have never witnessed before. This journey has taught me how to listen to God's voice within me. I never knew when these Writings started what was going to happen. I simply had to learn to stop over analyzing things in my life and just let it flow. By listening to the voice, letting go, and just writing as the thoughts flowed in my mind, I have learned how to see all the joyful moments around me every day with no stress, no worries, and no concerns.

God's gift back to me for letting go is a lasting peace with extraordinary joy. He has blessed our family with amazing grace filled moments like we have never experienced before. He has given me a front row seat in witnessing the best of God's design... All of you and this experience. I am writing about that discovery. Developing my Core provided the foundation that I needed to fight this illness. Learning to surrender and to trust God provided me an opportunity to win the biggest battle of my life.

The decision to stop the chemotherapy was easy and difficult. The decision was easy because of what the side effects were doing to my body. The decision was difficult because it shortens the time I have left with all of you. The first round of chemo consisted of two drugs given to me on Day 1 and then again on Day 8. I think Brock said it best when he said, "Dad, I thought you were going to sail through this chemo as you had already endured the most intensive chemotherapy for three months when you battled the lymphoma." I responded, "Yes. I was kind of thinking that too. I greatly under-estimated how weak my body was coming into the treatment and how hard it was to fight without a colon."

••••
178

The lymphoma treatments took almost two weeks before the freight train side-effects hit me. I had gotten four chemo drugs back then on just the first day. This time to combat the bile duct cancer, doctors only gave me two drugs on Day 1 of treatment. Their side effects hit me right away on Day 2. When they gave me the Day 8 course of chemo, I got hit even harder with side-effects on the same day. The medicine ripped apart my digestive system. The nausea, which was at first controlled with a cocktail of four different nausea medications, hit me without warning. I was immediately incapacitated within 30 seconds. After the Day 8 course, I developed acid reflux burps that scalded and scarred the back of my throat. It was painful to talk or swallow. Chemo brain set in fast. My thinking ability slowed significantly. My short term memory was limited. I was unable to talk coherently.

I was experiencing side-effects that were not supposed to happen. The neuropathy in my feet returned. I was not supposed to have any hair loss, but my hair started falling out easily. One of the worst side effects from my lymphoma chemo treatment, mucositis, started to surface when brushing my teeth. It felt like I had acid in my mouth. Even with all of that, I did not fully appreciate how my body really felt because I was being pumped up with a daily dose of steroids. I was receiving IV doses of a pain medication called dilaudid. One dose of dilaudid was like receiving 3 to 8 doses of morphine depending on your body type and how you responded to it. After the chemo started I was receiving 3 to 3.5 doses of dilaudid 3 to 4 times a day. That combination of steroids and pain medications was giving me a false sense of where my body was physically, until I came home.

• • • •

I wanted to protect my quality of life for as long as possible. The swift negative side-effects were robbing me of that chance. I was only half my strength when I was supposed to start Round 2 of the chemotherapy. The current chemo treatment was only going to extend my life by months. It was going to kill or incapacitate me faster than the cancer. I knew if I continued with the six rounds that were facing me, all my quality of life would be gone. I was not going to be able to do as much as possible for Kathryn, the kids, and my family and friends. No one knew what the chemo was going to do or how my body was going to tolerate it. We had to try. We also had to stop. It is now truly in God's hands.

Have I given up? No. Never. It is not in my DNA. I am prepared for anything that might happen. I asked my oncologist though to just give me his best guess at life expectancy. It is an impossible and unfair question. I am his first patient to have these specific combinations of cancers. When you throw in my other medical history nowhere do any meaningful comparisons exist to base an answer on what might happen. He tried to answer the impossible by guessing that I could have as short as four months to a little longer than a year to live. I thanked him and said with a smile, "Now I have something to try to beat!"

As the cancer progresses, I pray for the strength and understanding of the wisdom of God to endure and embrace whatever comes my way no matter the amount of pain or suffering, no matter the direction. I can honestly say since I learned how to fully surrender and trust that I cannot remember my last bad day, and every day I have been able to find joy, incredible joy.

I recently had a conversation with a woman I never have met face to face. She told me how these Writings

• • • •

have changed her life. She is a different person now. This type of conversation is what I have been witnessing for almost two years. The best kind of daily miracles. They are present every day. What was required on my part to see or hear them was learning how to open my eyes in the right way. Those opportunities can be easily created. Focus on others. You then see random acts of kindness as a result of putting yourself out there with a genuine desire to touch someone's life. To others it feels like God put someone in their life at just the right time when they needed that kind word, that kind act. It is what our family has experienced from you. Thank you for creating the little miracles in our lives. Thank you. Thank you for being you.

I love movies. I mean I really, really, really love getting lost in a movie. I enjoy the storyline, the passion, the emotion, and those great endings. *It's a Wonderful Life* is my personal favorite. Wow. When I reflect on my life now, it resembles some of the best movies. My life has an incredible love story. I have had lots of laughter throughout memorable moments. There have been fun adventures with family and friends. Dreams have come true. Championships have been played. Soaring faith-filled moments have been lived. My life has had health challenges and numbing drama. Inspirational experiences have occurred with lasting motivation. There have been heart-stopping twists over the years. My story has been a '*Wonderful Life*' with now an unimaginable ending. By the way, it was written by the best screenwriter ever - God. May God bless you, your families and friends always!

Love you from the center of my heart and soul,

Jerome

Happy Advent

(A note from Kathryn)
Sunday, December 2, 2012, 9:00 PM

Dear Friends and Family,

Just wanted to wish you all well this Advent season and give you a very brief update on Jerome. Many of you have asked Kathy how we are doing, have stopped me in passing at school or at church, and I realize that it has been a long time since we have sent an update to you. We are doing OK. Each day is a blessing, and we are grateful for all your prayers and support.

As we prepare for Christmas, we have remembered many fun times over the past 30 Christmases together. Setting up the tree this year brought back lots of fun memories. I love all those homemade ornaments! We still smile and search for the pickle. This year we searched long and hard only to realize that Brock had put it back in the box and placed it in Jerome's study on the shelf! Now if only the Elf on the Shelf would stay on the tree we would be ready for Christmas! We hope you have had some laughter and shared some fun memories with your families as well.

Jerome continues to take one day at a time. He struggles with pain (abdominal and rectal) and trying to get the right medicines and dosages to relieve his discomfort. Jerome has had the permanent rectal tube for the past 5-6 weeks. The tube is uncomfortable and requires a lot of flushing, but the good news here is that Jerome is not going in and out of surgery each week, as he had experienced from mid-September to mid-October. Fortunately he is off the 'liquid-only diet' and has found some foods that agree with his system!

● ● ● ●

Frosted Flakes and potato chips are right up on top of that list!

Jerome's spirit remains strong and positive, for the most part. He is amazing. He worked with my sister Julia and our friend Valerie for a week at the end of October filming videos for the kids. Another friend of ours, Jamie, filmed Brock while he was home over Thanksgiving to add to the mix. The footage they put together is fabulous. Jerome is now focusing his energies on his Writings. He is at his best in the mornings, tires easily, naps when he can, and is ready for bed in the early evening most days.

Jerome has managed to get to a couple of Gretchen's, Vince's and Audrey's basketball games (Once a coach, always a coach!), and yesterday he even managed to get to a Duke game and talk with player Ryan Kelly (Thank you Mrs. Casey!). He was thrilled. We have been blessed with visits from dear friends and family this fall. With the three kids playing basketball right now, I am keeping busy trying to keep our daily activities in check. I have been very grateful to the carpool fairies and Monday and Wednesday chefs helping to make my week a bit easier. For those of you who have given of your time, recipes, gas, food, prayers, cards, and many other efforts. Please know how much we appreciate all you have done. What blessings you are to our family. God Bless you as we "Prepare Ye the Way of the Lord" (A favorite from *God Spell*)!

Love,
Kathryn

• • • •

Joy of Life - Live, Laugh, Love
(A note from Jerome)
Wednesday, December 19, 2012, 12:30 PM

Dear Family & Friends,

Live, laugh, and love.

Live each day with the true real grace and kindness overflowing from a personal passion that simply warms all those who feel your presence. This day built from profound wisdom could be your last.

Laugh with genuinely deep belly laughs born from getting lost in life moments with people who can put smile after smile on your faces. Allow yourselves into each other's souls.

Love with pure penetrating emotion straight from our hearts. Create memories for one another wrapped in the best kind of generosity that is fed unconditionally.

May the incredible spirit of Christmas fill your life with lasting joy that comes from our faiths and cherishes all life from God. He gave us the greatest gift of all - Christ in one another. No day is an ordinary day. Live. Laugh. Love.

May God bless you, your families, & your friends with his love, peace and grace,

Jerome

Let Me Help You Through This Day
(A note from Kathryn)
Friday, March 8, 2013, 7:45 AM

Good Morning Friends and Family,

This was the *Jesus Calling* devotion from yesterday, "Let Me Help You through This Day!"

Wow! God certainly helped us through the day! I am grateful for the people God placed into my day yesterday - in presence and in prayer!

Let me start by saying Jerome asked me last night to send a note to let you know briefly (!) what is going on and where we are in our journey together. The last several months we have had ups and downs, surgeries, ER visits, and challenges that a life with an illness reflects. We have felt your prayers. We have appreciated all the cards, food, and kindness that you have continued to share with us. Most of all, your presence in our lives have allowed us to witness Christ among us.

A couple weeks ago, Jerome was hospitalized for nine days (blockage), a new rectal tube was placed, and the decision was made not to pursue any more surgeries - just replace the rectal tube as needed. We met with Hospice and got on board this past week. The nurse was set to check in on us once per week, and we were going to try a new pain medicine to help with the rectal and abdominal pain Jerome was experiencing. That being said, someone from Hospice was here Thursday, Friday, Saturday, Sunday, Monday, and Wednesday. Some of the problems appeared to be medicine related, so we were planning to go Thursday

••••
185

to reduce the dosages and find the right 'fit' for Jerome's pain and give him some relief.

Life changes. One needs to adapt.

Jerome and I went into the hospital late Wednesday night with complications, cramping, and pain. It was determined that he had a large obstruction, and the rectal tube was no longer functioning well. We needed to revisit the issue of surgery. Thursday it was clear that we had some major decisions to make. They were not minor or desirable choices; however, through much input and pure necessity, Jerome entered surgery late Thursday afternoon to have a diversion and ileostomy put into place. It was a major surgery - and a surgery Jerome never wanted to revisit. With Jerome's extensive medical history, nothing is ever routine. We truly put this surgery in God's hands. Joan and Jacques were with me through the day and evening.

Jerome's surgeon shared with us after surgery that our decision was the right thing to do. The blockage was large. We feared that with the number of blockages Jerome had experienced and the size and condition of this blockage meant that a perforation was a significant possibility. All in all the surgery went well. We all are hopeful that as Jerome recovers, we will have overall less chronic pain. The rectal tube is out☺, and the secondary tumor in his stomach that was blocking some of the bowel, has been reduced in size through the surgery (a portion was removed). Bottom line... We still have cancer. The diagnosis remains the same... biliary duct cancer. Cancer appears to still be evident in the liver, the secondary tumor site, and there may be evidence in the pelvic area as well. We were in ICU last night. Jerome's color was good, and he

●●●●

was resting when I left him around 11:00 PM. We are most hopeful that the pain will be less for Jerome.

I am on my way up to the hospital now. Please keep praying for:

(1) Reduced pain overall (surgery site, catheter)
(2) Strength to heal body, mind, and spirit for us all
(3) Patience and Understanding of life with the ileostomy
(4) Brock's safe travels home from Notre Dame tomorrow (Spring Break!), continued grace-filled moments together as a family, and cherished time together with our friends.

So, today's devotion in *Jesus Calling* says, "Save your best striving for seeking My face... Seek Me first and foremost... Then the rest of your life will fall into place, piece by piece."

As your pieces come together today... Praise God.

"For all things are possible through Him who gives me strength!"

Peace and Love,

Kathryn

Daily Progress Note
(A note from Kathryn)
Sunday, March 10, 2013, 8:00 PM

It is Sunday evening, and we returned from Mass with praises of Thanksgiving in our hearts. We spent the afternoon with Jerome, his cousin Kristy, and a few friends.

Jerome is doing much better than we ever imagined. His NG tube was removed late this afternoon. He is taking walks around the hospital. The epidural is helping him breathe deeply. He is still on water and ice chips, but is dreaming about eating real food sometime soon! His voice is strong and energized! I look at him and cannot remember the last time he sounded this strong. I realize that he is on pain medication, and I am thrilled that it is allowing him relief. Vince says, "It's nice to have him back!"

The girls and I just found out that we have no school tomorrow so we get extra time with Brock!

Thank you so much for your specific prayers. Sleep well☺.

Have a blessed week.

Kathryn

Joy of Life - A Beautiful Life and Woman
(A note from Jerome)
Thursday, May 2, 2013, 11:15 AM

Dear Family & Friends,

This special note today goes out to...

The love of my life...

The woman of my dreams...

The incredible mother of our children...

Happy Birthday, Kathryn!

Please join me in celebrating this beautiful life and woman today by sharing your birthday wishes with Kathryn in person or sending them in an email. It will light up her day with fun filled thoughts. Of course, I am in big trouble☺.

Since I am already in trouble, I wanted to bring a solemn promise to your attention. Many years ago Kathryn made me promise never to surprise her with anything on her 50th birthday. Today, I maintain that promise to Kathryn as she is exactly one year shy of that magical milestone. I guess others will be left on their own to figure out when that 50th milestone will be☺.

Happy Birthday, again, Dear.

Love you with all of my heart,

Jerome

● ● ● ●

An Update
(A note from Jerome)
Thursday, May 2, 2013

Family and Friends,

Thank you for all your thoughts, prayers, meals, carpool rides, gifts, etc. over the past several months as we battled through a very tough health period. As you heard in Kathryn's updates in March, we unexpectedly and suddenly got to the point where we found ourselves in a life or death situation. Emergency surgery was really the only option. I just barely got off phone calls to each of our children and my mother before they wheeled me back for surgery to begin. The stage 4 tumor had slowly grown and was squeezing off a part of my intestine above the pouch.

The recent trip to the Hospice Home in April for nine days was to find the right solution for pain control. Following the emergency surgery and the removal of the epidural and other IV pain medications, my pain reached a level that it had never been over the last three years. In April I was incapacitated daily with intense brutal pain in my tailbone that would not relent. The Hospice team developed a 4 page spreadsheet of medicines and frequency of delivery procedures for day and night. I started to get relief and began walking again at the Hospice Home several times a day. I was feeling better than I had in a long time.

Some fun notes. On the third day at the Hospice Home, I set off a nine alarm fire drill. My nurse thought I had wandered off and was lost. They sent out a search party, but I had just gone over to the chapel to pray and say a rosary without realizing I was supposed to let someone know where I had gone.

The next day Dr. Sutton came in my room and shared with me that she had been talking to the staff about me being one of the most remarkable patients that they have ever had. They could not believe how much pain medication they were giving me, how lucid and coherent I was, and how my body language just did not seem to reflect the pain I was obviously in. I smiled and shared with her the *Joy of Life* Writings and how what they were seeing in me was pure genuine joy that just overwhelmed any challenges or pain I might feel. It was a great discussion.

My appetite has come roaring back. Having my appetite back has been great. I had hit a low point just shy of 110 pounds in March. The nurses and staff have had fun calling me the Cookie Monster as I eat up all their little packages of cookies with each meal. I have gained weight since surgery with the ostomy working extremely well.

For the first time in months I have started to do some things at home. I owe my deep thanks to Kathryn, family and friends, my doctors, the surgery. Being able to eat regular foods and having a successful pain management program (that seems complete enough to treat an elephant), has allowed me to be a part of the family life again.

Thank you for all your prayers. I really feel them. May God's blessings be with you and your families to feel and live with the joy only He can provide.

Love, Jerome

• • • •

Summer Joy
(A note from Kathryn)
Wednesday, June 5, 2013, 8:15 PM

Happy Summer!

It is official. The kids are home and out of school, and we are ready for some good times together! I wanted to send an update and to thank many of you for wishing me a happy birthday at Jerome's request in May. It was wonderful to hear from you.

As I read *Jesus Calling* yesterday (When I started writing this note), it said, "Welcome Challenging Times as opportunity to trust ME. You have Me beside you and My Spirit within you, so no set of circumstances is too much for you to handle." Amen to that!

Let's go back a few weeks to share some exciting events here... many are answers to prayers. Jerome was well enough to participate and make some of the kids' and Jerome's bucket list items come true: mainly-Note Dame and Indian Princesses Weekends at Camp Seafarer.

Jerome shared with me that Brock wanted to walk on the Notre Dame campus with his dad one more time. Jerome had visions of coaching his boys playing basketball at The Rock on campus. Thank you Bruce for making this a reality!! Bruce came and drove Vince and Jerome up to Notre Dame in luxury. They were in a Suburban with wide comfortable seats and a DVD player! The day before they left, Brock got word from his ROTC Commander that he had the opportunity to fulfill his naval requirement cruise in Pearl Harbor! He would fly to Hawaii from South Bend while Jerome and Vince were still on campus! Brock went - had a great

••••

time and is now home. He loved the sub, but still thinks he might like to fly helicopters. I do not think I could last long in a sub... the 20 minutes I spent on Disney's 20,000 Leagues Under the Sea ride in the 1970s was about all the undersea adventure I could handle! Then again, the Dumbo ride leaves me with questions about the whole helicopter experience as well! I am thrilled that Brock had such a fabulous time in Hawaii! It is a blessing that he is home for the rest of the summer.

Jerome, Bruce, Brock, and Vince had an incredible time at Notre Dame together. So many people made this experience possible - I know I will miss a few, and I am sorry. We were so very grateful for Nancy and Peter Kilpatrick, Tom Campbell, Pete and Helaine Campbell, Head Basketball Coach Mike Brey, Father Hesburgh, and everyone else who were special angels in coordinating this phenomenal trip. The boys got to scrimmage with some ND players at The Rock, tour the stadium and locker room, and talk with Coach Brey. Brock, Vince, and Jerome had the opportunity to read from the *Joy of Life* with Father Hesburgh. What an honor!

Having a father and sons' weekend at Notre Dame was such a special gift. Before Brock left for his naval assignment, he and Jerome spent a night of prayer and reflection at the Grotto. Thank you to those you generously gave the Notre Dame gifts! The flag will be displayed proudly in the Friedman home (we will need to rotate it between all the children's bedrooms... It is in high demand!). Thank you to each of you! Many dreams came true and cherished memories were made because of your kindness. I know the boys will remember the time with Jerome always.

●●●●

Jerome came home exhausted from the long car trip to and from South Bend. His lab work was not the best, and he was very weak, but he was determined to join Audrey's Indian Princess Tribe for Spring Outing. Mary Grace and I drove down to get Jerome a little early so that he could get some much needed rest. We are very thankful to the rest of the tribe for watching over Audrey so that she could enjoy the camp activities with her friends.

The following week, after a blood transfusion, Jerome entered Hospice again and stayed a week to regulate his pain medicines. He was much more jaundice and his lab work suggested that his liver was really having a hard time metabolizing his large amounts of medication. Jerome was communicating a lot; I just was not able to understand most of what he was saying. That to me was very scary. While he was at Hospice he appeared to be acquiring what looked like bedsores. We soon learned that he had a large abscess on his bottom. They treated the sores with antibiotics, got the pain meds on a strict schedule, added a catheter, and put Jerome on his dilaudid pump 24/7. He came home last week on Thursday looking and feeling a bit better. His back side was a main source of pain.

Friday Jerome's nurse noticed that his port-a-cath site in his chest had a hole developing in the skin - meaning the site was contaminated! Yikes! The nurses informed us that they could come to our home to temporarily relieve the problem. They needed a room on the first floor with a door to close off the room where Jerome could lie down. Well, that ruled out the half-bath! Jerome's study would work, so Vince and Johnny (neighbor friend) moved 2 chairs out of the study and moved the couch right in. A vascular nurse

• • • •

194

arrived, portable X-ray service came, and a PICC line was placed into Jerome's neck (instead of his chest)! The nurse took an X-ray and did an ultra-sound. Flush, Flush, Flush and redo the X-ray. Did I mention that the X-ray tech had already wheeled all the X-ray equipment all the way back to the van already? So back into the house she came with her big fork lift type machine carrying the X-ray machine! The vascular nurse came with the biggest carry-on suitcase I have ever seen toting all the ultrasound devices and gowns. There were no sequins or pearls on these stylish gems, ladies! But all the activity certainly resembled a three-ring circus!

Finally, the PICC line was clear, Jerome was hooked up to the machine, and he was happy! This past Monday I took him in to the hospital to have the port-a-cath surgically removed. At that time, the surgeon took a peek at the abscess and said that it needed to be our number one priority. He opened it up to drain, and Jerome got some much needed relief. Jerome is thrilled to be able to sit again! It should heal up in 2-3 weeks. The port-a-cath and abscess sites look a bit like gunshot wounds. Let it be known, and I have witnesses that I did not create these wounds. Besides, I have better aim than that!

Jerome has had a good day today. His sister Luzann from Boston has been visiting. We have face timed with new babies in the family. And now with the kids out of school, we look forward to some game nights, *Seventh Heaven* marathons, and a few movie nights. Jerome has a list of things he wants to complete in the near future. He is almost done with his *Joy of Life* book. That is a big accomplishment!

• • • •

Life continues to move forward for us all. Vince is looking forward to working on his Eagle project this summer, Gretchen is heading to Myrtle Beach this weekend for a basketball tournament, Audrey is counting the days until her 9th birthday (only 14 more days!), and Jerome's birthday is June 26th!

Enjoy the fun and laziness of summer! Pick out a good book, sit back, and have a cool glass of homemade lemonade (I just heard John Tesh say that drinking lemonade makes you smarter! It is worth a try!).

We are so thankful for all the emails, cards, meals, treats, rides, and prayers that you have shared so generously with us. This journey has been long, and we are so blessed to have you with us along the way. Please know how much you each mean to us. Today's reflection says, "Closeness to Me satisfies deep yearnings and fills you with joy." Know that your presence in our lives brings us great joy - because you are the living Christ for us each day!

Peace and All Good Things,

Love,

Kathryn

Section Four
Jerome's Reunion

Chapter 13
Heaven Rejoices

(A final note from Kathryn)
Monday, July 1, 2013, 8:45 AM

Dear Friends and Family,

Heaven rejoices.

July has arrived and with it we are reminded of freedom. Jerome is free. Yesterday *Jesus Calling* talked of "Don't worry about what is on the road up ahead. I want you to find your security in knowing Me, the one who died to set you free."

Jerome died peacefully last night at 9:56 PM at our home. We had just said a family prayer of thanksgiving for Jerome's incredible example and presence in our lives. Although Jerome was sleeping, we all shared how much we loved each other, and we all said our good nights, our kisses, and our goodbyes. As suggested by Jerome's Goddaughter Erin, a candle stayed lit for the past several days, and the music of the St Francis choir and "Somewhere in Time" played soothingly in the background. Jerome was not alone. His brother Mark and I were with him... You all were with us in spirit as you have been every step of the journey. Praise be to God that his suffering has ended. As he left our home here on Earth, he literally had a smile on his face. That was a special gift to make the parting just a little easier. Truly the *Joy of Life*.

It is raining, and I take this as a sign from above that the angels are crying with great joy welcoming Jerome home. We, on the other hand, shed tears of

• • • •

joy for an incredible life well lived... but also sadness in our earthly connection to Jerome as husband, dad, son, brother, brother-in-law, son–in-law, Godfather, cousin, uncle, friend, coach, has now changed. He is in our hearts always.

Today, I read in *Jesus Calling*, "I am Life and Light in Abundance... By gazing at Me, you gain My perspective on your life. This time alone with Me is essential for unscrambling your thoughts and smoothing out the day before you."

As always, Praise God for His presence in our lives!

Love you.
Kathryn and the Friedman Family

Jerome's Obituary

Jerome Joseph Friedman. 52, died peacefully at home after a three year battle with colon cancer, lymphoma, and biliary duct cancer.

Jerome is survived by his wife Kathryn (his wife of 25 years) and his children: Brock(20), Vince(15), Gretchen(13), and Audrey(9) ; His Mother Louise(98) and his five siblings: Brother Paul Friedman, Mary Carol Williams (Dick) , Luzann Noonan (Larry), Mark Friedman(Mary), Joan Mistrot (Jacques). Jerome's nieces and nephews, cousins, and their families will also miss more special times with "Uncle Jerry". The Klein and Rosenow families also share in this great loss. Jerome will be missed by all who loved him: IBM, The Community of St. Francis of Assisi Church, Family, Friends, and the many athletes whose lives he touched.

Jerome was born to Walter and Louise Friedman on June 26, 1961 in DeKalb, Illinois. The Friedmans moved to Shawano, WI and then Rhinelander, WI. Jerome earned his degree in management from the University of Wisconsin-Eau Claire. After post-graduate study in Osaka, Japan, Jerome returned to the United States to begin work for IBM in 1984. Kathryn and Jerome were married in 1987. They lived in the Upper Peninsula of Michigan, Green Bay, Wisconsin, and Raleigh, North Carolina.

Jerome loved his faith, his family, and his friends. During his life and illness he learned to 'Let Go and Let God.' Trusting and Surrendering to God was a goal. He wrote about his faith-life journey in a book he called *Joy of Life*.

• • • •

Jerome loved his family. He told us he loved us often. He found joy in each day... and strived to make each day his 'masterpiece'!

Jerome embraced life. He thoroughly enjoyed learning with the people with whom he forged relationships. Jerome was a people person. He mentored many and learned from more. He enjoyed challenges and problem solving. He was a coach at heart. He was a life-long learner, and he wanted to share what he knew with others. He enjoyed chess, pool, golf, movies, and watching his beloved Green Bay Packers Football team. He loved to go to the kids' sporting events and help them improve their game. A highlight for Jerome was any opportunity he had to spend time with his family - especially the Friedman Family Reunions every two years!

Jerome loved coaching, faith, character development, and sports. He had passion. He studied and loved Morgan Wooten, John Wooden, Vince Lombardi, and Pistol Pete Marovich. He loved to see inspirational movies and use them to teach core values to his players.

He lived to exemplify the CHRIST principles that he developed working with other coaches.

- Caring,
- Humility,
- Respect,
- Integrity,
- Spirituality/Sportsmanship/Surrender, and
- Trust/Teamwork.

Those who walked with him on his faith journey understood his commitment to the Lord and his direction in life.

The family wishes to thank Dr. Mark Yoffe, Dr. Matthew Strouch, Dr. Ron Schwarz and the many nurses, nursing aides, patients, and staff at REX Hospital that made a difference in the treatment and care of Jerome while he was battling his ulcerative colitis, colon cancer, lymphoma, and biliary duct cancer. Wake County Hospice Care Team was a blessing. Thank you, Kezia and Lisa, for coming to the house often and taking the time to get to know our family. You made a difference!

We could not have made this journey without our faith in God, our family, our friends and the Community of St Francis. 'Thank you' does not begin to express the deep gratitude we feel. We rejoice in God always!

Visitation with the family will be at the Gathering Space at St Francis of Assisi Catholic Church, 11401 Leesville Road, Raleigh, NC from 6–8:00 PM Monday July 8th.

A Mass of Celebration will take place at The Catholic Community of St Francis of Assisi, Raleigh, NC, 11401 Leesville Road, Raleigh, NC on July 9th at 1:00 PM. Interment to follow in the St Francis Columbarium. Please join us to celebrate Jerome's life in person or in prayer.

Chapter 14
Jerome Friedman's Celebration of Life
July 9, 2013

Presider: Father William "Bill" McConville, O.F.M.
Co-Celebrants: Father David McBriar,
          Father Brad Metz
Musicians: John Angotti, Jim Wahl, Jenn Fiduccia

First Reading ~ Ecclesiastes 3:1-4; 10-14

There is a time for everything,
And a season for every activity under heaven:
A time to be born and a time to die,
A time to plant and a time to uproot,
A time to kill and time to heal,
A time to tear down and a time to build,
A time to weep and a time to laugh,
A time to mourn and a time to dance.

I have seen the burden God has laid on men. He has made everything beautiful in its time. He has also set eternity in the hearts of men; yet they cannot fathom what God has done from beginning to end. I know that there is nothing better for men then to be happy and to do good while they live. That everyone may eat and drink, and find satisfaction in all his toil - this is the gift of God. I know that everything God does will endure forever; nothing can be added to it and nothing taken from it. God does it so that men will revere him.

Second Reading ~ Philippians 2:1-5

If you have any encouragement from being united with Christ, if any comfort from his love, if any fellowship with the Spirit, if any tenderness and compassion, then make my joy complete by being like-minded, having the same love, being one in spirit and purpose. Do nothing out of selfish and ambition or vain conceit, but in humility consider others better then yourself. Each of you should look not only to your own interests, but also to the interests of others. Your attitude should be the same as that of Christ Jesus.

Gospel ~ Luke 24:13-16, 23-25

Now that same day two of them were going to a village called Emmaus, about seven miles from Jerusalem. They were talking with each other about everything that had happened. As they talked and discussed these things with each other, Jesus himself came up and walked along with them; but they were kept from recognizing him.

They went to the tomb early in the morning but did not find his body. They came and told us that they had seen a vision of angels, who said he was alive. Then some of our companions went to the tomb and found it just as the women had said, but they did not see.

●●●●

Words of Remembrance
By Vince Friedman

Thank you. Thank you for being here today. It means a lot to our family to have you here.

Jerome Joseph Friedman is the person we have all gathered here at St Francis to remember. You may know him as Jerry, JJ, Coach Jerome, or other nicknames you called him from points in his life. His sister Joan called him Jer Bear.

This afternoon I would like to share with you words that describe the person I know and simply lovingly call my Dad.

Coach - As a coach, my dad has touched my life and the lives of many others through the game of basketball. He was always there, guiding us to be the best players that we could be. One thing that was very important to him was not only forming us to be good basketball players, but making us into great men. Over the years, he was having us master the skills of basketball, but even more important to him, was constantly using opportunities to build our character and instill the knowledge vital to our success in life.

Honorable and Happy - Everyday people were touched by my dad's joyful attitude toward life. He always brought a smile to your face and enjoyed the comfort of your happiness. I was always amazed by his ability to have a positive approach to everything. My dad's choices mirrored his values.

Responsible - I could always count on my dad. The most important thing to my dad was trust. My dad

• • • •

once told me, "Trust is the most valuable thing you can give to someone." I trusted my dad and I maintained my trust with him. My dad always took responsibility for his actions. He was the first to admit his wrongdoing, yet he did not draw attention to his good deeds. My dad was dependable and trustworthy, he was somebody I wanted working on my side.

Intelligent - My dad was always the person I went to if I had any question about life, school, or whatever was on my mind. His answers would guide me to discover the right path to take. His intelligence was not limited to factual knowledge; he had a deeper understanding of moral and spiritual values. I began to realize as I got older that my dad was not just smart, he was wise. He applied his knowledge and understanding for the well-being of others.

Sincere - Whenever my dad said something, he meant it from his heart. He spoke truthfully. I knew that every piece of advice that my dad gave me was because he loved me. My dad was someone that I could depend on. I could always count on his word. My dad lived out his faith by keeping to his promise and following through.

Thoughtful - The thing that always amazed me about my dad was that he cared about everyone. Throughout my dad's life, he was always looking for an opportunity to reach out his hands to others. His acts of kindness were straight from his heart. He thought of others as much as he thought of himself. His thoughtfulness is a quality that I admire in my dad and want to emulate as I continue to grow and mature.

• • • •

As each day passes, I realize even more how much of an amazing person my dad truly was. I was so blessed to have been his son and learn from his example for 15 years and I am proud to call him my dad.

Words of Remembrance
By Brock Friedman

Thank you, all of you, for coming out here today. By being here you are reaffirming the support that my dad promised would be here, and it is both comforting and reassuring. While my younger brother just shared how great of a father my dad truly was, I would like share another, equally important side of his life. My dad's faith life was the strongest of anyone I have ever known. I cannot imagine any other person who upon receiving news of a terminal illness goes and praises God. But that is exactly what my dad did. He lived his faith out loud through the CHRIST principles.

Caring - As Christians we have always been taught to care for others. My dad embodied this to the fullest. I learned how to care for others simply by observing how he treated them. In high school my dad would drive me to school sometimes, and he always waved to everyone walking by as we passed. I didn't understand at the time and was embarrassed, but he told me, "What if I am the only person who waves at them today?" He was just caring for others at the most basic level. That always inspired me to reach out to others.

Humility - My dad always strove to live a humble life, and he succeeded. But more importantly, he taught our family the importance of humility. As

• • • •

Christians we are not called to flaunt our possessions, we are not supposed to lavish in wealth. Rather we should appreciate what we do have, and be thankful. Be thankful for friends. Be thankful for family. And always remember that all of those things have come from God. My dad once told me that humility is the greatest gift of all, and that we should always remember how Jesus humbled himself and washed the feet of his disciples.

Respect - It is not our job to judge ourselves above others, or to even judge others. It is our job to treat others with respect. To embody the message of Jesus and treat them how we would want to be treated. Respect is one of those things that is hard to earn and easy to lose. I have nothing but the highest respect for my dad and the man that he is. He is a role model of who I want to become.

Integrity - My dad told me when I was little that, "Integrity is who you are when no one is watching." It is our true character regardless of the circumstances, not just when it's convenient. It's about being true to our faith and the teaching it gives us. When my dad gave his word it was better than a written contract, he stayed just as true to his word as he did his faith.

Surrender - Throughout this trying journey over the past two years, my dad has never wavered in his surrender of himself to God's will. From the first time he heard the word cancer to the last day he lay in bed, he never fought God's plan... He only embraced it. He knew that God had a plan for him and he followed it without hesitation or reluctance. He did not quit, he never gave up. Rather he realized that what God had in store for him was different than what he wanted. He accepted that.

Trust - Trust in God. If we are fully able to place our trust in God, there is nothing to fear. There is nothing to want. There only is the promise of eternity in heaven. My dad trusted God. Throughout this entire ordeal he never doubted his faith; he never second guessed the choice God was making. Finding the strength to trust God is not easy, but it was not meant to be. It serves as a way of solidifying your faith, fully places your life in God's hands. That is was trust is all about. Don't trust just when things are good and going your way, trust ever more when the opposite is true and the world seems against you.

My dad never thrust his faith upon someone or tried to convince anyone their beliefs were wrong. He lived what he believed. He did not have a gray faith, it was black and white. Look at the marble block, the principles shown, the foundation laid out, all of them embodied here. My dad served as my role model here on earth, and now I know he is my guardian angel watching over me from heaven.

Section Five
Eternal Joy

Dear Readers,

Jerome wrote these final thoughts during the last two months of his life. As he approached the end of his earthly journey, he continued to share his message so that you too could embrace everlasting joy.

Chapter 15
Joy of Life ... Joy for Life

Joy of Life

Have you ever seen a shooting star? It is amazing. The pure speed of it. In just a nanosecond, you see this brief flash of white light streaking across the sky. Faster than anything you have ever seen before. It makes everything else stand still against the night sky while it zooms by.

It lets you feel and imagine at that moment, when this brilliant white light is streaking across the starlit night, the enormity, the absolute enormity, of our universe. How small our earth feels at that moment. You feel the incredible distance the shooting star covers in that instant flash. It all adds up to something in our world that is breathtaking, captivating, exhilarating, and inspiring. Imagine light traveling at tremendous speeds in every possible direction in its feeble attempt to find the edges of our universe. In some cases that light never reaches the edges of our world, and in other cases it goes beyond what the human eye may ever see. Those thoughts help me realize how vast the universe is and how much we do not know. It is a humbling reflection.

Eternity. God. Faith. Faith has taught us that God has built an eternity for us. It is something honestly that I had never taken much time to try to comprehend. I had heard about it. Imagined it. A place in eternity with God - but it was in the future.

When you have a terminal illness, you see life differently. It should not take a death sentence to

••••

realize what is already there. Everything I see now has always been there. I just did not fully appreciate it or make the time for it. Creation. Faith. God. Eternity. Seeing the brilliant shooting stars recently brought eternity, God, and faith into a magnificent vivid focus. It is simple. Our life is not meant to be lived for ourselves. We are living for something so much, so much greater.

Every word we say and every action we take each day counts. It counts. God is real. Eternity is real. How we live each day is the true faith we are showing God. We do not fool Him with our intentions. He hears our thoughts. He knows how we love one another. How we treat those around us. I believe God offers us eternity with Him.

Calling it an offer does not do it justice. We do not fully come close to appreciating the best opportunity we will ever be given in our lifetime. Take a moment to reflect on what God is asking of us and what we receive in return. It is a gift beyond comprehension. He has told us one of the key determiners already. "Love one another as I have loved you." If you need rules, seek The Commandments. To me, the real secret is the unconditional love of one another. Do this right, and eternity is yours.

Imagine what it must be like to be a part of something that lasts forever. What is included with such an incredible gift? The feelings we will experience with one another, the new colors we will see, the parts of the universe we will be introduced to, the endless design of this gift from God we cannot even comprehend. It is all a part of the offer. Do you want

• • • •

to taste a few of the possibilities? Start with one... Watch a shooting star.

The best description of eternity I ever heard was to think of the earth as a giant steel ball suspended by a steel chain extended out into our universe. Imagine a hummingbird flapping its wings against that giant steel ball for ten thousand years. When that giant steel ball and its chain have turned to dust, eternity still exists. Unchanged. Amazing.

When I first heard this analogy, I just sat back in awe. I prayerfully reflected on my life, and whether I was prepared for eternity with God. It helped me visualize part of what eternity meant as a piece of my faith. It matters how we live out our beliefs. Our actions need to be consistent. We cannot just do *this* or believe *that*, and then live our lives differently. Who are we kidding?

I have said for quite a while now that if everyone knew and felt what suffering was, sin would not exist. Why? Who would take that chance to spend an eternity suffering? Can you imagine lasting suffering? Day after day. Week after week. Month after month. Year after year?

Is there any material prize on this earth worth putting an eternity with God at risk? No. You could offer me every gift possible on this earth in exchange for putting my eternity with God at risk. My answer is without hesitation, No. Nothing in exchange. Nothing even comes close to being worth it.

Think. There is a lot at stake. Sin is real. If you trust God, you ultimately surrender your control of

••••

your life to Him. God does ask us to trust Him. Fully trust Him. It is not easy, but it does not have to be complicated.

God gives us this offer of eternity and how He wants us to live. He asks us to love one another unconditionally. That means we must never judge. Ever. We judge when we label people. That is what we do when we use people. We judge them as less relevant than ourselves. We are better. "This is for me." "This will help me get ahead." How hollow is that? We live our lives in the best light by always bringing out the best in one another. We always accomplish the most when we work together. We solve real tough problems when we are honest and put others first in our thinking.

There are good questions to ask. How many lives? How many lives have you impacted in positive unconditional ways? Think about the converse of that. How many lives have you judged or ignored? What prize, what status, what victory would cause you to trade God's offer of eternity? This happens when we ignore God and live our life inconsistent with what we know to be the right way... The right way... God's way. My words and actions every day need to reflect my Core words and their definitions.

It does not need to be difficult. It can be simple. I know if I am living my life consistent in God's way. More importantly, so does God. That is it. We are the only two who know. God is the ultimate judge of eternity. He knows my thoughts. He knows how I treat people. He knows if I am doing the things in my life in order to spend eternity with Him. He is going to test my character throughout my life. Is the Christ

• • • •
218

coming out of me, or is the 'me' coming out through my actions? Which one does God see?

Embrace the challenges that come into your path. I believe it is God's way to further shape and chisel us to bring forth the Christ within us. He wants us to totally trust Him. We do that when we fully surrender everything to Him. The gift we receive in return is lasting joy. You can handle any challenge because you know there is a God... You trust Him... Completely... One hundred percent!

Faith. Faith in yourself. Faith in each other. Faith in God. Having faith in God means having full and complete faith no matter what life brings. God is always there even when things do not go well in life.

I cannot remember my last bad day. That is unbelievable to me. In the midst of the most intense pain and suffering, I have this deep, lasting joy day after day. Pure joy. No matter the circumstances. No matter the challenges. No matter the pain and suffering. It is there. Genuine joy that never fades. Pure joy does not turn on and off anymore but permeates every part of my day. This is the way I always wanted to feel!

You can experience joy when you start to view life through an outward focus on others. You realize that the 'me first' life needs to go. 'Me first' is where all the stress comes from. We start letting our lives center around serving ourselves. In fact, we do something that we never intended when we think and act this way... we, in effect, tell God that we do not fully trust in him. How can this be true?

• • • •

We stop someplace short of surrendering every part of our lives to God so we can retain some feeling of control to ensure the outcome we desire. If obstacles come into our path, they are dealt with. We either first try to just avoid them or at a minimum try to get them to behave as we would like. Others? Others many times are just enablers for what we want in life. Our joy is at our best it seems when everything in our lives is aligning and falling into place. When this happens, we feel joy. But, when things get out of alignment, that joy seems again to quickly fade until we find a way to try to get things back in alignment. We are discovering that our joy is more closely aligned to happiness than to what pure joy is at its core – unconditional love and living.

We do want true joy. It does make us feel great. We reach out to God to help make this happen. We pray to Him for this or that. When faith is honestly assessed, it is more than thanking God for the good things and asking for strength or different outcomes for the bad things. Trying to achieve a lasting joy becomes nearly impossible because life contains curve balls that we do not control. Doesn't it seem hard to get what we want when we want it? That is because life is God's design not ours. He is in control. We are not. He is asking for us to surrender and trust in His plan for us, and we struggle with doing that on all levels.

What is it that we are truly seeking? This is gut check time. This is the time to be completely honest with ourselves and the reality we are living. There is no wiggle room here if you are seeking lasting joy. The 'me' driven life has to go. There is no 99% in surrendering and trusting God. If you want joy that is

• • • •

always 'on', that just emanates out of every part of your fiber, whose strength enables you to get you through any challenge in life, then you have to make an upfront decision. I ask you, "Do you have a true genuine desire in your core to serve God on this earth by caring most for others?"

The words and actions you choose each day are key elements. Are you reflecting your Core words and their definitions with how you are living each day? When any challenge comes into your life path are you ready to accept it, even embrace it? You can when you are surrendering, trusting, focusing on others, and living out your Core in your words and actions. You can do this! Let God become your power source, the source of genuine joy that is always there and radiates from you. Life can feel like heaven on earth. Our life's goal now is the lives of those we encounter each day.

How do we do this? How can we get there? What are the power sources of lasting joy that never fade? Complete trust in God. Surrender 100% of the control of your life to Him. Put others first in your thinking. I have found these to be the three key power sources of everlasting joy. Begin with prayer. Your prayers help teach you how to learn to surrender and trust Him completely. Develop and believe at your core that you are in His plan. God does not make mistakes. None of us will ever fully understand His plan. If we did, "God" would be in our name. If we are kept in the dark, it is more for us to learn how to fully accept and believe without question. Everything and everyone put into our life each day is God's way of shaping us into His perfect image. We no longer need to waste precious energy trying to explain the reasons why this or that happened. Instead, we embrace the moment.

• • • •

We bring forth the Christ within ourselves. We use our Core words. We realize we are human, and there are going to be bumps and mistakes along the way. So be it. We keep smiling and embracing. We are not going to get discouraged or quit. We know about shooting stars and the incredible offer we have accepted. We have agreed to live our lives emulating Christ. God has a reward waiting that is unlike anything we can imagine for our efforts to live in this light.

Let each moment of each day flow through you. Learn how to let your words and actions come out with the Christ within you. How differently that makes you see the everyday twists and turns. How differently that makes you love everyone you encounter that day. You now are living in the moment. In fact, you wake up to a lot you were missing before. You now see this amazing creation that is all around us in so many incredible shapes and sizes. The difference in how you feel living this way is almost indescribable.

Please do not misunderstand me. Do not think for a moment that by letting life flow through you that you become lazy and control nothing. No. Rather you are just getting started. You still wake up every day bringing your best effort, your very best. You do control things. You do make things happen. You still have goals. You are now inspired to reach that absolute limitless potential in yourself as God designed. You are really living. We each are given an endless set of blessed talents. We each have our own set of unique gifts that only God fully knows. Our task is to keep unwrapping them for one another.

• • • •

When you live an outward focused life, when you fully surrender and trust in God, you begin to witness this amazing set of endless gifts we each can give and bring out in one another. Gone are feelings of envy. Gone are questions of why this person has gifts? Why some people are rich and I am poor? Why some people are smart and I struggle? Why some people are tall and beautiful and I am short with all sorts of scars and imperfections? We start experiencing lasting joy when we are focused on trying to bring out the best in one another.

Do we believe in eternity? If we honestly did, we would never sin. We would not want to do anything in our lives that would put at risk such an incredible opportunity. Eternity is beyond our wildest imagination. We can all bring out the living Christ within us in all that we say and do. Is this joy worth the effort? Yes! Yes! Yes! We can all have eternal joy.

I remember when Dr. Yoffe had delivered the tough news. The stage four cancer tumor was most likely terminal bile duct cancer. That afternoon the palliative care nurse stopped in to talk with Kathryn and me. "He looks great," she said. "Oh," I said. "You see my spirit. Would you like to know how my body feels?" She twisted her head a little to the side looking back a little puzzled and said a drawn out, "Sure." I went on to describe the intense amount of pain at various points inside my body. I told her where I was agonizing in pain right at that moment. She looked back at Kathryn and said, "Wow, he hides it so well." I quickly said, "No, I do not hide it. I feel every ounce of it. It is just that the joy, the pure joy I also feel right at this

• • • •

moment, overwhelms it. That is what you see on my face."

The nurse affirmed the incredible gift of genuine joy from God that I have experienced. It emanates from every ounce of fiber I have. First, I fully and completely surrender to God. Second, I trust Him and His plan for me without any question marks. No matter what life's path may present. Third, I live my life by focusing on others first. Fourth, through my Core word list, I strive to be joined and strengthened by the Christ within, emulating God's teachings in my words and actions each day.

Thank you, God. Thank you.

• • • •

Joy for Life

Joy.   Real, lasting joy is the joy that lets you meet any challenge, any news, or any twist or turn in life.

This joy comes as a result of learning the full meaning of obedience – trusting, surrendering, and listening to God in our weakest most challenging moments. It is easy to be obedient and to trust when things are going well. It is a totally different thing to do it when your world is crashing in upon you. News that never seems to go your way. Life experiences that are crushing in the intensity of suffering that do not relent. What I came to realize was that I had never fully trusted God before. I had always been reserving some control for myself. When you fully trust and learn what it means to fully surrender to God, there is a reward that is as immense as the universe. There is calm.   There is peace.   There is strength. There is nothing that life can put in your path that you cannot handle. You see life in the way we were always meant to see it. You now see the shooting stars in your life. Why? How? It has an incredible benefit.

You bring forth the Christ within yourself by how you live your life.   The person you are. The character you represent.   The choices you make.   How you treat everyone. The love we are taught is unconditional. This means in its raw form that we love everyone without judgment.   We realize they too are being chiseled by God. Who knows? Maybe God is asking us to help shape them by how we love them and make them feel. It is one thing to love those you enjoy being with, it is another thing to love the most repulsive looking, rude, insensitive, irritating, vulgar person you ever met. This is a good place to start because after

• • • •

that, the rest is easy. You may get a positive response. Do not ever act with expectations, because they reduce your sincerity and your genuineness in random acts of kindness. When motives, words, and actions become solely about the other person, it will be better received. That is simply Christ's way.

I think this is what the Saints mastered by living in the same way Christ did. They became so in-tune with the Christ within themselves that they just kept bringing it forth day after day, moment after moment, regardless of the circumstances or persons they encountered that day. In time they became living Saints - modeled, shaped in Christ's image with the uniqueness that God created for each of us.

Peace comes when we give control to God. What does that mean? Does that mean we do not bring a Vince Lombardi or John Wooden effort to every day? No, not even close. The key is to understand that you are not in total control of your life. Things are going to come into your life every day that will challenge you at various levels, from minor inconveniences to major life-altering, leg-numbing news and events. How do you see these things when they happen? Do you let them frustrate you? Stress you? Fill you with worry? Do you react by hurting those around you with your words or actions because of your rising level of frustration with what is happening? Find peace in your life by bringing your best every day; That will allow you to manage any challenge life brings.

I built my reputation, on two things - integrity and execution. I was never going to break my word, and I never confused activity with results. It was all about getting things done. It did not matter how long it took,

••••

or how short it took; it was about getting it done right. If I could do something in 10 minutes, that took other people hours, then I did it in 10 minutes and used the rest of the time to do what else needed to be completed. If the task took hours, I would take the time needed to finish the project. It was not just the result. It was not just the execution. It was doing the right thing.

When my son Brock was in second grade, he learned the saying, "When you work together, you accomplish more." I have found this to be true on most occasions. When I added even just one additional person, I achieved a better result. I had wonderful roommates in college. I would ask them opinions on assignments, papers, life challenges. My roommate junior and senior year was a journalism major. It did not matter how well I wrote something or how well I thought it was done. I would give my paper to him, and when he gave it back to me, it was better. It was just that simple. When you work with someone else, better things happen. When you think only about yourself, you constrain yourself and limit your opportunities. Life is not the destination. Life is the journey. Accomplish greatness.

I think what made IBM great was the reputation of getting things done. If IBM made a promise or a commitment, you had faith that IBM would do whatever it took to fulfill that agreement. That was why many people chose IBM as a business partner or as an employer. It was a safe decision. Customers knew they were not alone to work through and solve problems. That was what made me such a great salesman. It was not that I was so articulate. It was not that I could sell better than anyone else. No. It was that I built genuine, trusting relationships that brought something of value to the person or to the company. It was that simple. I became a great salesman by helping people and focusing on others.

I remember the biggest deal of my career. There were multiple sales meetings. We lost several of the preliminary rounds, and then our time came. Through our immense efforts, we got the deal. It was going to be a great partnership with the company. I had pulled in multiple vendors (long before IBM had started doing any kind of compound, custom deals). We were right on the forefront. It was going to become the premise of what business is today.

We put the letter together of our commitments to take to the customer. We included everything that we said we were going to do. I remember one section, however, where the team at Headquarters said, "No, we cannot guarantee that." I said, "But that is what we committed to." Headquarters said, "No, we cannot do that." Ultimately, headquarters overruled our letter to the customer and forced the change.

Well, I knew right then and there that the whole deal was at risk. It seemed insane to have worked that hard, to build our business' reputation on trust and character, and then throw it all away. We were investing in the customer, trusting and getting to know one another, and believing that our words meant the truth. In this situation I had to put something in writing that was not reflective of the deal that I had agreed to with my customer.

I carried the newly written letter to my customer as confidently as I could. I knew it was not right. As the

● ● ● ●

customer read the letter, he responded, "This is not what we agreed to." And I said, "I know." The person from headquarters who was with me quickly said," Well what do we need to say?" I knew what we needed to say; we just did not want to say it. The letter had been changed. We lost the deal right there.

Unbeknownst to me at the time, the customer was getting pressure from his company to change his original decision and not sign with IBM. Because of his trust in the relationship we had developed, he was willing to put his faith in me as a business partner. He was willing to go with IBM. We did not know that he had been pressured immensely. I firmly believe he never would have changed his decision. He would never have changed his mind; he would have followed through on the commitment we agreed upon in that original document. He believed in me and I believed in him. He would have lost his job before he would have changed his decision based on our trusted relationship. I gave him a clean path to back out of the commitment when I handed him the changed letter. We lost the deal, but I gained a respected friend.

That is how precious a commitment is. That is how precious a promise is. We need to live our lives in a way that shows people that we can be trusted. When we make a mistake, we are honest about it. Apologize. Ask for forgiveness. Accept apologies. Forgive. Then move on. Learn from it. Do not keep repeating the same mistake. That is not forgiveness. That is neglect.

Back to my story, IBM headquarters eventually decided to change the letter back to what the customer originally had agreed upon. IBM realized that the

• • • •

original agreement was a favorable decision. Well, you can imagine the response when we took the original text letter back to the customer. It was too late. Just like life, it is too late sometimes. You know the right thing to do, but you fall short, you stop yourself from fully doing it. What is the price you pay? The price you pay is lost opportunity. Much effort is now needed to rebuild something that was right there, that was given to you. You tried to manipulate it. You tried to get around it. You fell short of what you knew you were supposed to deliver because it was going to be easier, quicker, or you never intended to do it in the first place. Maybe you were hoping that someone would forget what you were supposed to do. That is not how you build relationships. That is not how you build trust. That is not how you build a reputation of integrity.

I have guarded my integrity as the most sacred thing in the world to me. I rarely say I promise. When I say I promise, there is nothing that I will not do to fulfill that promise. I learned that lesson early in life when I broke promises. I made promises, but I did not keep them. Breaking a promise was a formula for disaster. That was a formula for ruined relationships. Someone once said to me, "The truth is so much easier to remember than a lie." My life has been very simple, because I only deal in the truth. I only speak the truth.

The words that we choose to say to one another are powerful. Realize what a precious gift our ability to speak and to communicate with one another is. When we speak to one another, let us not spend any time on negatives. Let us fill that time with joy, love, goodness, caring, concern, enjoyment, happiness,

• • • •

humor, and all the positive things we can think of. Yes, we need to work through differences. That is what compromise is about. Can you imagine a marriage without compromise? Can you imagine a family without compromise? Can you imagine a business without compromise? Compromise is how we learn. Compromise is how we grow. Our children are always asking questions. Can I do this? Can I do that? Why not this? Why this? That is how we grow, that is how we educate, that is how we teach, and that is how we learn. But if we speak back to others with judgment, with criticism, or with prejudice, we do not build positive relationships.

How do we make each other grow closer to one another, understand each other better, love one another more? Whether you are Christian, Muslim, Buddhist, Jew, Shinto, or whatever, live the example of your leaders. Look for ways of working together and of compromise instead of engaging in conflict and destruction. Reap the goodness. Reap the love. Reap the peace.

My days have been so filled with joy. I cannot remember the last day I had without pain and suffering, but I also cannot remember any day that has not been more filled with joy. Why did God put this pain and suffering in my life? I think to wake me up. To use me to help others wake up. To use this voice to raise others and myself up to a higher spiritual level. That is how we are designed - To help bring out the best in each other. That is what fills you with joy. When you feel that genuine joy, you see everything differently. You see people differently. You see situations differently. You see many opportunities. Life becomes incredible every moment. You can look

● ● ● ●

anywhere and see the joy of living. In the midst of suffering, you can feel the joy of living. That is what it means to truly trust and to truly surrender to your faith.

I learned to surrender. I got the news that I had a third cancer, a cancer that would take my life. I remembered how I had beaten the lymphoma. I had surgery to take out colon cancer. I had struggled with ulcerative colitis for over eighteen years. I called my mother this time to share with her the latest health challenge. I said, "Mom this moment, this moment right now is when God puts my life on the table and asks me, 'What is the depth of your faith?' "

What is the depth of your faith? How much grayness is there? I do not want a gray faith. I want it to be strong. Full trust. Full surrender. What did God give me in return for that? He gave me peace. He gave me a peace that is so indescribable. I saw joy in the faces of people who brought my food or cleaned my room; I saw joy in the nurses that cared for me; I saw joy in the doctors who tried everything they could think of to save me. I saw the best in people. We just do not tend to see these things when we let poison slip out of our mouths - whether judgments, criticisms, prejudices, or destructive hatred. We start to see things differently. We miss so many opportunities to see the joy that is always there.

I have seen miracles since this journey began. I mean real miracles. I do not think it is coincidence. Divine intervention? Maybe. Maybe that is how God works. I do not know. I guess I will soon find out. I wish I could share with you what I find. No, what I think I have come to believe is that we create the

●●●●

miracles! We do. We create the miracles with one another by how we act, how we think. How we treat one another. How we love. How we forgive. How we make someone laugh. How we put a smile on a kid's face. How we put an extra bounce in someone's step. That is what we are given each day. Opportunities. Each moment. We create the miracles for one another.

I will give a fun example. My brother called me last week to see how I was doing. When the phone rang, the first thing I heard was, "Guess where I am?" followed by, "It's your favorite place in Wisconsin." I said, "Lambeau Field? You're at Lambeau Field?" He said, "No, even more favorite than that." More favorite than that? What is better than that in Green Bay? Let me think. And I replied, "Dina Mia Pizza?" He shouted, "You got it!"

Dina Mia Pizza is by far my all-time favorite pizza in this entire world. It is located in Rhinelander, Wisconsin, in a small building off Woodland Drive. I grew up on that street. When my mom and dad would go out to play bridge or get together with friends at church, my sisters and I would get to order a Dina Mia Pizza for dinner. Holy cow! I thought I had won the lottery, because that meant not only could I get a pizza, I was also allowed to have one soda. I could have one pop - that was a precious commodity. Boy, you know if we had Coke, Wow! 7-Up, Woo-hoo! Of course, the downside was my sister's favorite at that time was Tab. I did not like the taste of Tab, but my sister loved it. Sometimes that was the only soda we had. I would think, "Oh, man," but I would drink it, because that meant that I could have pizza and a pop.

• • • •

So here my brother was at Dina Mia Pizza saying, "You know what I'm going to do? I'm going to get a couple pizzas, get them half-baked, freeze them, and then I'm going to carry them on the plane when I come down and see you in October." Wow! What a gift! There was a miracle right there. The opportunity to get Dina Mia Pizza that I had not tasted for over ten years delivered to my doorstep. You can imagine my excitement.

My brother called me later on in the week to tell me about his trip home. When he got out of the pizza place, he realized that he had come up to Rhinelander on his motorcycle. How was he going to get back to his home? There was not going to be much left of those pizzas after 60 miles on a motorcycle. While he was standing there, thinking about that problem, a young man, somewhere between 20–25 years old, came up and said, "Can I help you?" This young generation that we say is so off, so wrong, going in the wrong direction. No. Here was one young man who immediately offered help. He had some duct tape and some twine in his truck. Together they duct taped those pizzas and tied them on the motorcycle with some twine. The pizzas traveled 60 miles back to my brother's home to be put in the freezer for home delivery next month!

That, I submit to you, is a miracle. Created and done completely by people. It is within our power. It is within our control. We can do this. Take our country back? No. We do not need to take our country back. What we need to take back is our criticism. What we need to take back is our prejudice. What we need to take back is all of our judgmental behavior. What we

••••
234

need to take back is hate that we feel toward anyone or anything.

Let us start with ourselves. Let us hold ourselves accountable first. Let us get back to the person and the design that God intended for us, and let us remember how to live and bring out the best in each other. God did not design us to live for ourselves. He designed us to live for each other. He gave us the opportunity to create Heaven on Earth. He gave us the opportunity to create a miracle each day for someone, because we bring something of need at the right moment, at the right time to someone. That is the gift of our faith. That is the gift of any faith in this world. It is not that difficult. So the first thing we need to do is not to criticize this president, that president, that candidate, that country, that government, that religion, or that person. Oh my goodness. Listen to us when we do things like that. It is not how we were designed. No wonder we have problems. No wonder we have stress. No wonder marriages fail. No wonder children get abused. No wonder why there is crime. No wonder people do not trust one another.

We can change that. You can change that. Right now. This minute. Right now, forever. Change that lasts a lifetime. And what will be the rewards? You will have a life that will be stress free. You will not have another worry or concern in your entire life, ever again. But it starts with you. You have to want to really make this change, and make it last. Moment after moment. Day after day. For the rest of your life. Even if it is over tomorrow. Especially if it is over tomorrow. Realize how precious every day is. There are no ordinary days. There are no ordinary moments. Each one is really a gift. It is a gift! Trust me, it is a gift!

●●●●

Hear my voice! Hear in my voice how much I would love to have years to come. My cancer is going to take my life, so I can tell you this. Wow! It really magnifies those moments now. They are under the magnifying glass. They are under the microscope. I see so much better in life. I see people, and I see the goodness in them. I see the day, and I see it filled with opportunities. I see nature, and I go, "Wow! God, what a magnificent design! The beauty, the colors! How you intertwined it all! It is endless going out into the universe!" That is what I see every day. If you had that every day, how could you not also be filled with incredible joy? How could you not engage with the people that you meet in that day and just feel the goodness and bring out the best in one another? Let each other know you care and are here for one another. Say, "I will help you."

Do you need some tape or some twine to make a difference in your life today?

Here it is. Take it. Thank you.

I love you,
Jerome

Epilogue
Reflections on Joy

• • • •

Reflections on Joy

(A note from Kathryn)
Thursday, June 5, 2014, 5:10 pm

Dear Friends and Family,

The *Joy of Life* started as a dream. It had a purpose, and it is the beginning of a life journey.

The book was a dream. Jerome always wanted to write a book and share his insight with others. He was a natural coach and teacher, wanting to help others reach a goal. He felt the Core words were critical to developing potential. It was not until he faced incomprehensible health challenge after challenge; It was not until he was stripped of all the securities of the earthly existence; It was not until he completely surrendered to God and fully trusted in Him, that his mind opened up to share the message that he felt destined to reveal in the *Joy of Life*.

The book had a purpose for Jerome. Initially, the purpose was to share the Core words and the concept of their development. Then the purpose was to share the journey of his faith through illness and the joy he found when he let go and let God. When the illness or treatment became too much to handle, the book was there as a distraction. The book allowed an outlet for him to think freely and express raw emotions, fears, joys, successes, and failures in life. The book provided a place to journal and explore Jerome's mission on earth. The book gave him a voice to share information about life with Brock, Vince, Gretchen, Audrey and his family now and for future generations.   Jerome's Writings and Core words allowed him to communicate and connect with those around the world - people he

••••

knew and people he had yet to meet. His message was clearly bigger than himself. He made a difference by sharing it with others. Jerome's purpose became more than the pages of this book. The concept of the *Joy of Life* morphed into a perspective on how to live life to the fullest.

The Writings served a purpose for me as well. The Writings documented our time together. As we walked together through the surreal experience of Jerome's illness, our life was a blur. We took a day at a time as the demands of the illness controlled our every moment. Anyone who has gone through an illness of any degree knows how it affects the family. Ours was no different. We stayed connected to family and friends for support through the *Lotsa Helping Hands* website. The Writings provided a journal of this time and memories to cherish as we go forward.

Jerome's story was a journey. At first, navigating the chemotherapy and hospital stays was the destination. Then it became the challenge of the multiple surgeries and balancing medical treatments. When we knew that we had no more treatment options, our goal became an incredible testimony of faith and trust - not only for Jerome, but for many of the people who read his Writings on the internet. People spoke and thanked Jerome for the impact his Writings had made in their relationships and in their lives. He would explain that most of the time, he did not know for sure where the thoughts or words came from, but he felt God's presence in the delivery. Jerome knew it was important for him to relay the message. He learned about himself and his faith as he walked this path. For Jerome it led him toward surrender, trust, and joy.

• • • •

For all of us, our journey begins where Jerome's journey left off. It continues for a lifetime. He challenged us to choose our Core words carefully and live them out in our daily lives through our actions. Quoting John Wooden, Jerome would continue to encourage us all to, "Make each day your masterpiece!" As I spend time with this book, I am glad that Jerome left us with a voice and such direction for our lives.

How do we journey with the joy Jerome has described through difficult times? This past year has been a year of change. Three weeks after Jerome's death, Granny Lou, his ninety-eight year old mother, died. Five months later, my dear grandmother who raised me, died at age ninety-seven. All three 'Rocks' in my life were stellar examples of who I wanted to be. They believed in God. They believed in others. They believed in themselves. Experiencing much joy with all three of these special people over my lifetime was a gift. Losing all three of them in a short period of time was incomprehensible. Do I miss them? Definitely. Do I wish I had more time with them? Of course. Do I imagine their laughter, their smiles, their conversations and wisdom? Always. So how do I go forward?

I continue to run the race as though to win. I get up in the morning and thank God for my children, my family, and my friends. I am grateful for the gifts I have been given and try to use them to make a difference in someone's life each day. I choose not to let my past define my future. My focus is joy. Finding joy in the quiet moments. Finding joy in each other. Always finding joy in the Lord. He is there for each and every one of us. With Him all things are possible. With

• • • •

hope and faith, I will finish the race. I pray that God will be pleased.

It is June once again... A month full of celebrations: Father's Day, Audrey's 10th birthday, Jerome's birthday, and Jerome's first anniversary in Heaven. Last year we purchased a grill on Father's Day so that Jerome could have a ribeye steak grilled to perfection! He loved steak. Jerome celebrated his 52nd birthday at home. He had his favorite Goodberry's strawberry shake, and he blew out the candles on his always requested homemade German Sweet Chocolate Cake. Four days later, Jerome joined all the angels in Heaven. He was a firm believer in praying the rosary daily. How fitting that his birthday celebrations on earth and into Heaven were on the Glorious Mysteries. In honor of the joy Jerome's life brought to us, we celebrate the birth of *Joy of Life* this month as well. This book and Jerome's message have given us something to look forward to.

We thank you for your continued prayers and presence in our lives. You have allowed us to grieve, rejoice, heal, and continue on our path together.

Keep sharing the memories with one another. We have all shared in Jerome's story. He has left part of himself with us. We will never be the same.

Do not postpone joy... Live it!

God Bless.
Kathryn

Jerome Joseph Friedman
"Coach"
(June 26, 1961 – June 30, 2013)

••••